OLD & NEW

KATHERINE SORRELL

OLD & New

RYLAND
PETERS
& SMALL

LONDON NEW YORK

First published in the United States in
2002 by Ryland Peters & Small, Inc.
519 Broadway
5th Floor
New York, NY 10012
www.rylandpeters.com

10 9 8 7 6 5 4 3 2 1

Library of Congress Cataloging-in-
Publication Data

Sorrell, Katherine.
  Old and new : combining past and
present in contemporary homes /
Katherine Sorrell.
     p. cm.
  Includes index.
  ISBN 1-84172-318-5
  1. Antiques in interior decoration. I. Title.

NK2115.5.A5 S67 2002
747--dc21   2002021380

Printed and bound in China

COMMISSIONING EDITOR Annabel Morgan

LOCATION AND PICTURE RESEARCH MANAGER
Kate Brunt

PICTURE RESEARCHER Emily Westlake

PRODUCTION Deborah Wehner

ART DIRECTOR Gabriella Le Grazie

PUBLISHING DIRECTOR Alison Starling

contents

INtRODUCtION

For most of us, decorating is not a question of taking an empty room and filling it with brand-new coordinated furnishings; nor is it a case of inheriting a matching set of priceless antiques. Usually, we're somewhere in the middle—a couple of hand-me-downs here, some chain-store pieces there, perhaps a few things picked up in a secondhand store, maybe a special item we've saved up for. And then, of course, our homes are constantly evolving—things wear out, or go out of fashion; we get bored with them, or they're no longer useful. The old-and-new approach to decorating is simply a realistic way of tackling these challenges, of celebrating the eclectic mix that surrounds us, and of creating a beautiful, comfortable, characterful response.

Combining old and new, sometimes in a seamless, harmonious blend and sometimes in a dramatic and surprising juxtaposition, can be done in any room in the house. Here, we've used the living room, bedroom, kitchen, and bathroom as examples, but there's no reason why you shouldn't extend the principles to a hall, sunroom, or home office. Wherever you try it, however, there are endless variations. Your scheme may be based around one precious piece, surrounded by relatively neutral furnishings, or it may be more diverse, blending all sorts of items together in an intriguing, eye-catching way; it may contrast period architectural detailing with 21st-century sofas and chairs, or place 18th- and 19th-century antiques in an ultramodern interior; it may take a single color as its starting point, or an ethnic theme, or perhaps retro style. What's for sure, however, is that every scheme will be unique and individual.

There are no hard and fast rules to combining old and new, but it's worth following a few guidelines, which are set out in this book, along with plenty of wonderful photographs and detailed text. I hope the result is exciting and illuminating, and that it inspires you to be bold, imaginative, and experimental, creating rooms that are as much a pleasure to be in as to behold.

spaces

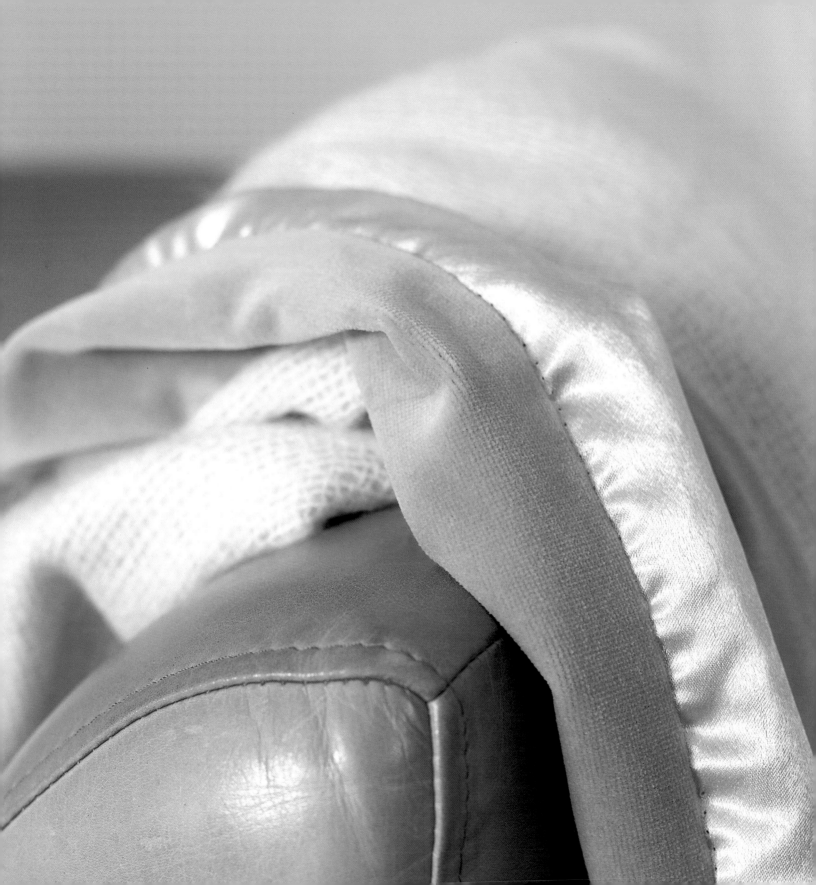

LIVING

A mix of old and new pieces can create a living room that is both elegant and eclectic. By pairing new furnishings with older pieces that have developed a pleasing patina of age, you can create a balance in which textures, colors, shapes, and styles combine and contrast beautifully, and where subtle harmonies and dramatic differences result in luxurious and relaxing rooms.

THIS PAGE AND OPPOSITE **This welcoming room effortlessly combines old and new. The deep, inviting sofa is upholstered in classic leather, but possesses simple modern lines; a cozy fireplace is set into a chic recess; plain walls and a bare wooden floor are offset by fashionable accessories such as velvet-covered pillows and a luxurious satin and mohair throw.**

reLaxeD moDerN

OPPOSITE The white walls and pale floor of this Paris apartment emphasize the feeling of space. Classic Le Corbusier armchairs mingle happily with flea-market pieces.

LEFT, ABOVE In a converted barn, modern sofas and chairs are counterpointed by an old storage cupboard with visibly worn wood.

LEFT, BELOW This may be a period property, but the laidback, pared-down decorating style is entirely contemporary in its simplicity.

RIGHT These capacious armchairs have been reupholstered in vintage wool blankets to create an inviting place for relaxation in a minimal London loft.

The marvelous thing about mixing old and new is that the result is a wonderful combination of the laidback and the impressive—an interior that is both enjoyable to be in and a pleasure to behold. By introducing antique, retro, or salvaged furnishings into a modern environment, you will instantly tone down any harsh lines, add a dash of warmth to cool colors, and introduce the appealing characteristics of the aged, the worn, and the well-loved. The overall look can be as contemporary as you like, but the addition of just one or two old pieces will provide the necessary air of easygoing repose and mellow pleasure.

The starting point for relaxed modern is always a sense of space: a modern aesthetic can never be achieved if there is too much clutter. Airy, light-filled rooms are ideal, but if your living room is dark and poky, there are plenty of ways in which to increase its potential. Paint the walls a pale, muted color and use light-colored flooring, either pale wood, carpet, or natural matting; you could also consider pickling or painting dark floorboards. Minimize window treatments, using just the simplest of curtains or shades, or perhaps even getting rid of them altogether. Make

RIGHT Pieces from very different eras sit happily alongside one another in this relaxed room. The fireplace has an almost medieval feel, topped by a classical medallion, while the armchairs are modern, covered in hard-wearing denim.

BELOW This London apartment is calmly contemporary in warm neutral shades. The mix includes modern suede-covered pouffes, a classic armchair, and a 1930s Doulton Acid jug.

OPPOSITE Pickled wooden floorboards and a plain, almost austere backdrop give this London loft a pared-down, contemporary feel, in spite of its period furniture in worn leather and chintz fabric. This look is inexpensive and easy to recreate, and relies on lack of clutter and the impact of spots of color in a light-filled room for its effect.

sure that anything unattractive or inessential is stored out of sight, so that you create as much space as possible and the focus is only on useful or beautiful objects that you love to have around.

With these bare bones in place, you can consider your furnishings. The one essential is a capacious couch or, better still, a pair of them. The sofa can be either old or new; if old, make sure it doesn't have any uncomfortable broken springs, or worn or torn upholstery. Old sofas, especially in leather, can have a delightfully aged texture, but sometimes recovering, in hard-wearing plain cotton, velvet, or bouclé, results in a great improvement. Again, pale colors (although impractical if you have children or pets) tend to emphasize a contemporary aesthetic. Alternatively, you might prefer an armchair or two, large enough to curl up in, or even a chaise longue, which will inevitably add a note of languid elegance to the most pared-down of interiors.

Because plenty of storage is important, you may find that an antique chest or cupboard or an old cabinet or sideboard makes a useful addition to the mix. A blanket chest or footlocker makes a superb contrast with minimal, modern furnishings, for example, while a lean, low 1950s sideboard would ideally complement their sleek lines and slim styling.

ABOVE **The eclectic pieces in this airy Paris apartment all share a similar sense of quality and craftsmanship. While they date from several different periods, they share a clarity of line that means they look just right together.**

LEFT If you come across a tacky old sofa in a secondhand store but don't want to go to the trouble and expense of having it reupholstered or making a slipcover, do as the owners of this Dutch home have done, and swathe it in cream linen (or cotton) sheets, tucking them in at the sides and around the edges. The wrinkles and creases contribute to the easy-going, laidback look.

Or, for an impressive focal point and a distinct change of tone, opt for a more decorative piece such as an antique French armoire with carved detailing, or an old English hutch with distressed paintwork.

When buying old or antique furniture, look out for well-made pieces in good-quality materials and simple, understated colors. Natural materials have their own innate integrity, so are always superior to synthetic ones. In a living room, the seductive textures of heavy grained wood, cool stone, patinated leather, and crisp cotton or linen will combine to create a reassuringly timeless atmosphere. Combining these materials with shades of white, cream, taupe, stone, and gray makes for relaxing surroundings, although it's important to include occasional splashes of color— perhaps some old chintz made into pillow covers, a vintage blanket used as a throw, some smoky 1970s glassware, or a bold 1950s block-print poster. In general, it's best to limit the number of accessories; displaying just one or two carefully chosen pieces that express your interests or personality, whether

they are centuries old or date back only a few years, will result in an appealing effect and an entirely contemporary feel.

Last, but not least, consider the way in which lighting can alter your living room. Discreet low-voltage downlighters set into the ceiling are almost invisible, casting enough light for reading or writing and to showcase prized ornaments and pictures. They can be supplemented with attractive period fixtures that possess more character, such as a classic gooseneck lamp or a simple Edwardian-style silk shade, perhaps with beading around the edge. And don't forget that the soft, flickering glow cast by candles is the most restful and flattering light of all.

When putting together a relaxed modern look, it's essential to balance the elements that will soften and relax with those that are more formal and structured. With the right choices of old and new, your living room will possess an enviable mix: the grace of the past with the sophistication of the present.

ABOVE In this converted church in London, the living space offers a gently welcoming atmosphere, thanks to the warm colors of the wooden floor and furniture, and the restful simplicity of the repeated motif of horizontal and vertical lines. Old church chairs sit happily beside a modern daybed and a robust retro coffee table with chrome legs.

RIGHT Steel roof trusses have been left visible in this modern extension to a converted gasworks. The industrial ethos is echoed in the pitch-pine flooring and hanging metal lamps, but is softened by several rugs, a country-style dining table and chairs, and a classic gooseneck lamp.

LEFT The textural contrast of a faux-fur pillow adds a dash of glamour to a classic armchair.

LEFT, BELOW A touch of gold, in the form of an eighteenth-century French chair, livens up a room with a muted palette.

RIGHT With the mirror as a focal point of this room, the Georgian-style sofa has been plainly upholstered so as not to clash with it. A mid-twentieth-century chair introduces another point of interest without being too distracting, the middle tone of its wood complementing the dull gold of the mirror's frame.

OPPOSITE The floors and walls of this living room provide a neutral backdrop for a strong theme of blue and gold. The twirly legged coffee table and glass accessories have clearly been chosen by the same feminine decorative eye.

gold and glamour

Whether the aim is to create an interior with plenty of impact or to achieve a feel of subtle luxury, nothing beats the glamour of gold. In small quantities, gold adds understated elegance; in larger quantities it brings high-voltage opulence and drama.

You only need one splash of gold to make this style work, giving your living room a bold focal point while the rest of the furnishings are quietly complementary. For an eye-catching look, choose a piece that is oversized and ornate. A huge gilt-framed mirror, for example, can be propped against a white wall for a vivid contrast in color and texture. Keep the rest of the surroundings simple—painted floorboards rather than thick carpets; Roman shades rather than dressy swagged curtains.

If your style isn't quite so minimal, it's possible to mix and match a few pieces that share similar attributes—a curving gilt-legged table, for example, will sit happily alongside another item that has the same attention-grabbing qualities, such as curvaceous Murano glass or an elaborate antique chandelier. Just don't go overboard, or the effect could become clumsy rather than covetable.

THIS PAGE An eclectic mix of pieces from different periods sits well against the plain walls and floor of this living room. Curving shapes are a repeated motif, while muted colors and the absence of pattern mean that the furnishings harmonize perfectly.

FAR LEFT These velvet-covered French Art Deco armchairs have a rich, sumptuous feel that complements the lines of the modern coffee table.

LEFT The gaping hole of an empty fireplace can be a problem; but here an antique candelabra fills the space beautifully.

BELOW An all-white room provides an excellent backdrop for glamour. Simply add a single oversized, eye-catching piece such as this heavily carved antique gilt mirror.

For a more subtle look, mix textures and colors that give an impression of understated luxury. Choose fabrics such as velvet, silk, faux fur, and metallic organza, and shapes that twist and twine in an intricate fashion. Elaborate carving, in small doses, adds to this look, particularly when contrasted with relatively minimal surroundings, as do decorative elements such as beading, fringing, patterned rugs, and Venetian glass mirrors. Splashes of deep, rich color—berry reds, midnight blues, or chocolate browns—against a pale background will create an atmosphere of indulgence. Clever touches such as these needn't cost a fortune, but will come together to create a living room that possesses dreamy, divine glamour in endless abundance.

RIGHT This loft apartment has an almost industrial architectural structure, with bare white walls, exposed brickwork, and a white vinyl floor. But it has been furnished almost entirely with pieces from the mid-twentieth century, from the plywood Eames chair of 1946 in the foreground, to the 1950s Jacobsen dining chairs on the right, to the 1960s Castigioni-inspired floor lamp. The seating on the left is also distinctly 1960s in flavor, while the sideboard and sunburst clock are typical of the 1950s. The result is an eclectic mix that is fresh and appealing.

FAR LEFT The plain, flat front and tapering splayed legs of this sideboard are quintessentially 1950s. The objects on display are mid-century, too, but the overall feel is more modern, thanks to the contemporary prints on the wall above and the shiny vinyl flooring.

LEFT Although this 1950s sofa is minimal enough to be modern, the two table lamps that flank it are very much of their time. Use quirky pieces such as these with discretion, as they make a big impact. Here, they work well as the only decorative flourishes in a room that is otherwise totally pared down.

retro inspired

Furniture and accessories produced in the mid-twentieth century have a distinctive energy and optimism all of their own. Such pieces, whether celebrated modern classics or unassuming pieces by an anonymous designer, have become increasingly popular in contemporary homes, complementing modern schemes in a way that is attractive, easygoing, and full of character.

Retro style can encompass designs from the 1930s through to the 1970s, but, for a fresh, simple look that is easy to put together, seek pieces from the 1950s and early 1960s. Sofas, chairs, and sideboards from this era are slimline and clean-cut, raised off the floor on spindly, splayed legs; colors are fresh and clear; and accessories such as clocks, vases, and lamps tend toward the quirky and eye-catching.

To create a retro-inspired living room requires only one key piece, though many people find that once they have bought one item they become fascinated with the period and simply can't stop. A long, lean couch is a good start: either an expensive version by a well-known

LEFT The traditional character of an old-fashioned wood-burning stove contrasts with a pair of burnt orange armchairs by British designer Robin Day. This room is filled mainly with lucky secondhand finds.

BELOW In the same room, an array of ceramics and glassware from the mid-twentieth century, with typically whimsical outlines and vivid patterns, offers a dash of drama.

RIGHT A double-height ceiling and expanse of plain white walls in this converted office building on the outskirts of Paris allow a pair of retro-style armchairs, recovered in navy velvet, to flaunt their shapely forms.

designer such as Florence Knoll, a re-edition by a major manufacturer, or a lucky secondhand find that needs reupholstering. Integrate it into a contemporary room by keeping the surroundings as plain as possible—bare boards, parquet, or rush matting are best for floors, while white-painted walls allow the distinctive silhouettes of these pieces to stand out. Sideboards and armchairs from the period are key pieces, too, as are spindly lamps with conical shades. If your living room is large enough to incorporate a dining table, you could offset it with a set of typically 1950s Scandinavian chairs.

Retro pieces will integrate well with modern furnishings in a 21st-century living room, thanks to their pared-down, delicate designs. They also make a fabulous statement in a period home, standing out against molding, ceiling details, and paneling as an unexpected contrast. More eccentric accessories, used with care, add splashes of color and fun. After all, this is a look that doesn't take itself too seriously, but creates a mix of old and new that is fresh, individual, and enjoyable to live with.

gLObaL fusION

Just as mixing old and new sets up exciting contrasts and combinations, combining pieces from East and West creates similarly intriguing juxtapositions. Whether you introduce contemporary Chinese-style seating into a period living room, or make ancient Oriental artifacts the focal point of a modern loft space, a fusion of global styles from a variety of periods is a unique way to bring character and interest to any home.

This look works best when the color scheme is based around intense shades such as crimson, chocolate, or indigo, which have the ability to transform a living space into an inviting cocoon. If you prefer a lighter look, simply use a single element of dramatic color combined with white, taupe, gray, or another neutral shade.

In many Eastern cultures, homes tend to be furnished far more sparsely than ours and feature seating that is

ABOVE AND OPPOSITE **This Yorkshire chapel was originally built in 1834. Today, it has been converted into a home, but still retains its original stone pillars and wooden floor. The modern Oriental-style furniture (above) seems initially to create a stark contrast, but in fact, its simple, angular lines perfectly complement those of the building. The result is a calm and peaceful space, given an injection of warmth and drama by the vivid red cushions that top the chairs and benches.**

close to the ground. By removing extraneous furnishings and accessories and choosing low-level seating, you will instantly make a start toward creating a distinctly global look. For impact, choose furniture with strong forms or ethnic designs—an Oriental-style chair with a solid, square shape, perhaps, or an African "throne." Either would make a striking contrast with European furniture from any era. Dark woods, brass, and cane are all typical materials, and very different from 21st-century pine, concrete, and stainless steel.

Adding global artifacts is another good way to inject diversity and eclecticism. An African sculpture or woven basket, Indian saris made into pillow covers, an antique Turkish kilim used as a wall-hanging—all can be used to introduce an element of the exotic. When aiming for a pared-down, zenlike feel, use just one or two favorite pieces; for a more dramatic, rich, and embellished style, combine items old and new from around the globe and create an intriguing interior that has immediate warmth and unabashed personality.

LEFT This modern vase has something of an Oriental flavor. Its simple sculptural shape is highlighted by the dark-wood antique screen behind it.

RIGHT, ABOVE AND BELOW This tranquil living room is decorated in predominantly neutral tones, with two red-painted walls that add vibrancy. The furniture combines new and old, East and West, with simple, spare shapes sitting side by side in a seamless mix. There's no grand focus to this room; instead, everything is quietly comfortable.

OPPOSITE In a very old Paris apartment, red-painted beams immediately create an Oriental atmosphere. The modern modular sofa has the right kind of long, low look, complemented by an antique ethnic chair and coffee table, both quite rustic in style. A hard floor, with an intriguing inset pattern of octagonal tiles, completes the picture.

LIVING: GETTING IT RIGHT

★ Keep it simple—don't try to cram too much furniture into a living room. When mixing pieces from different periods, you only need a few examples or the effect will be cluttered.

★ When you have one very strong pattern, keep the rest of the furnishings plain, avoiding clashes and allowing the pattern to make a dramatic statement.

★ For the lines of furniture to really stand out, keep wall treatments understated and pale in color.

★ Old chairs, from whatever era, look marvelous reupholstered in white or off-white fabric. Alternatively, have slipcovers made, for a more informal look.

★ Lengths of old fabric can be made into pillow covers. Against a plain backdrop, florals, toiles, and 1960s prints look great, adding plenty of character and color.

★ For old furniture to work with new, both should have a similar feel. Keep them clean-lined and pared-down, and look for shapes that echo each other, such as gently curving lines or boxy silhouettes.

* Remember that scale is important. One overscaled piece will make an impact, but avoid mixing lots of large and small pieces in one room—it will look crowded and cluttered. This goes for the details, too: if a table is average in size, but has heavy, square legs, for example, it will look wrong next to a chair of similar proportions with slender, tapering legs.

* To avoid causing visual confusion, keep accessories to a minimum, choosing a few quiet, timeless pieces, or just one bold item.

* Use color to coordinate: if a piece of wooden furniture is not working with the other elements of your living room, try painting it the same color as the walls. It will then blend in better.

* Look for good-quality furniture that has a timeless style. Excellence in design, a high standard of craftsmanship, and solid, natural materials provide common factors that unify different pieces, whatever their age.

cooking & eating

The kitchen and dining room provide ample opportunities for pairing the traditional with the contemporary. Modern appliances look good contrasted with old-fashioned implements, while new dining tables can be mixed with old chairs, and built-in units can be offset by quirky period pieces. Enjoy the harmonies and juxtapositions between shapes and colors to create rooms that are chic but relaxed, the warm and friendly heart of a home.

OPPOSITE, ABOVE In this raw, urban kitchen, a quirky mix of old and new is emphasized by dramatic lighting.

OPPOSITE, BELOW In this 1930s Antwerp apartment, many of the original fixtures have been carefully preserved. This dining room has a beautiful original parquet floor and paneled walls, but the modern lamps, bowl, and minimal shade provide an unobtrusive contemporary twist.

LEFT In New York's SoHo district, a former loading bay has been converted into a comfortable modern home. The rough brick walls, inset with wooden beams (to prevent damage from trucks), provide a contrasting backdrop to a chic contemporary dining table and chairs, while the finishing touch is a sleek wall-mounted stereo.

RIGHT Plain white walls and a grid of black-and-white photographs add chic modernity to a kitchen made from reclaimed lumber, which also features an old-fashioned ceramic sink and salvaged and restored brass faucets.

URBAN SOPHISTICATION

Whether you live in a 21st-century loft, a Federal townhouse, or an Arts-and-Crafts apartment, a casual mix of old and new is an ideal way to soften the hard edges of city living, bringing uncontrived warmth and individuality to an urban dining room or kitchen. Using contemporary furnishings and smart detailing makes it easy to create a sophisticated room that looks impressive and effective, but adding older materials, furniture, and accessories will bring the space to life.

The key to this look is texture—every bit as essential an element as color and form. Contrasting textures can be understated or dramatic, but are always satisfying, bringing an indefinable pleasure and sense of satisfaction to the look and feel of a room. To combine textures requires some consideration, but is not overly difficult. Balance hard against soft, pitted against smooth, matte against shiny, and the result will be enjoyable and enriching. When using old and new, this comes completely naturally: rugged brick

LEFT A set of classic
Arne Jacobsen dining
chairs, with slender steel
legs and wooden frames
is in perfect harmony with
a simple, modern, wood
and metal dining table.
Each has a quality that is
quietly distinctive, shown
off beautifully by the plain
walls and floor.

RIGHT AND OPPOSITE
Handy open shelving
and displays of stylish
accessories and
foodstuffs help soften
the sleek modernity of
angular built-in units.
Well-loved and frequently
used pots and pans not
only look attractive, but
are also within easy reach
for cooking.

walls against fabric-covered dining chairs; sleek stainless-steel work
surfaces against rough plasterwork; a grainy wood dining table with a
plastic hanging light, and so on.

High-quality materials and workmanship are essential for a chic city
kitchen or dining room. Rustic finishes simply won't do; instead, tables,
chairs, cabinets, and surfaces should be sleek and well turned out,
functional but also beautiful. If you are teaming a set of 1950s dining
chairs with a modern table, for example, make sure each one has its
own integrity of form, so the two looks harmonize rather than clash.

Finally, add a selection of accessories, perhaps an old industrial-style
lamp hanging low over the table, or a French enamel sign on the wall,
a few contemporary photographs in symmetrical rows or simply a trio
of clear glass vases—finishing touches that encapsulate the subtle yet
carefully thought-out combinations that make this look so attractive.

LEFT Lots of light and a spacious layout give this kitchen a contemporary feel, which is emphasized by the cream-painted built-in units that run along one wall. High stools and an old woodworking bench with simple, square outlines add a more traditional element, as does the lovely set of old-fashioned weighing scales.

ABOVE This sophisticated wood veneer wall treatment has a timeless quality that is offset by traditional faucets, a 1930s clip-on spotlight, and good-looking kitchen implements.

ABOVE RIGHT Pared down to the bare essentials, this calm kitchen features scrubbed floorboards, freestanding furniture, and an old-fashioned refrigerator. What's more modern is the white-on-white color scheme, which gives a minimal-meets-rural effect.

FAR RIGHT Even with fairly new built-in units, this kitchen has a country style, thanks to the unusual swan-necked faucet and, especially, the traditional checkerboard ceramic floor tiles. The casual assortment of objects on display adds to the effect.

contemporary country

A kitchen decorated in country fashion doesn't have to be twee or traditional. Putting a more contemporary spin on country decor creates an interior that still possesses all the ease and relaxation that makes this look so appealing, but with a fresh, modern edge that is a delight to live with.

The important thing to remember about the modern country kitchen is that it shouldn't look too "fitted." Naturally, you need plenty of storage and workspace, but that doesn't mean bland, square units and laminated counters. Instead, mix modern built-in elements with an old hutch or butcher's block, a freestanding side table with a low shelf underneath, or simply rows of open shelving.

Some materials are more suitable than others. Knotty pine, for example, tends to look dated and cottagelike, although other good-quality woods have a lovely appearance that softens and warms a room. Painted wood gives a country feel without being old-fashioned and is an excellent way of disguising less-than-perfect pieces. Stripped original

LEFT Even in a kitchen with modern built-in units, it is entirely possible to create a country effect. Simply add open shelving on which to display rows of teapots or other items, poles or hooks from which to hang saucepans and general implements, and a large table around which are grouped a set of mismatched chairs.

LEFT, BELOW This relaxed kitchen features enviably capacious storage cupboards with roomy drawers beneath to hide away any clutter. A comfortably large dining table, in sturdy, plain, country style, is matched by a lovely old set of simple wooden chairs. The bold modern print on the wall provides a counterpoint in terms of both color and style.

RIGHT When space is at a premium, folding tables and chairs are extremely useful. This kitchen is full of cozy clutter, but still retains a contemporary look by virtue of the plain paneling of its painted cupboards and the neat arrangement of storage jars and dishes on the open shelves.

OPPOSITE A cheerful yellow shade dominates this simple kitchen, in which built-in cabinets are combined with free-standing appliances, and neat rows of stainless-steel canisters contrast with the rough surface of an old dining table.

floorboards are the ideal flooring, while ceramic tiles are the most practical solution for the walls above sinks or work surfaces. Touches of cane and metal are useful additions to the textural mix.

Overall, aim for a feeling of light and space. Hang Roman shades or sheer voile at the window to allow in plenty of sunlight, and keep walls and floors plain. Furniture, although sturdy, should be simple, and accessories kept to a minimum, so that each piece adds impact rather than getting lost in clutter. Glass-front cabinets are better than ones with solid panels for maintaining an airy, open feel. And, finally, keep displays on the formal side—if you have open shelves, it takes some discipline to maintain a tidy appearance, but neat, well-spaced rows of pans, boxes, or ornaments demonstrate an easygoing country aesthetic combined with a more considered contemporary style.

OPPOSITE This kitchen has a lovely balance of materials. Old wood and steel predominate, but the white tiles, while subtle, marry the two together.

FAR LEFT Upholstered chairs temper what would otherwise be a hi-tech kitchen, adding comfort and softness to the straight lines and hard metal elsewhere.

LEFT, ABOVE AND BELOW Metal-clad cupboard and drawer fronts contrast with a wooden worksurface.

BELOW These old and new free-standing kitchen units don't quite match, but nevertheless possess the same good-looking and hard-working qualities.

WOOD AND steel

A combination of wood and steel almost invariably looks good; the gleaming, reflective nature of metal provides an ideal foil to the more traditional elegance of grained wood. It's a mix that works particularly well in a kitchen, where the necessity for lots of hard, rectangular planes means that it can be all too easy to suffer from monotonous surface textures. The addition of a contrasting material makes all the difference, creating interest, personality, and sophisticated appeal.

There are plenty of ways in which to mix wood and steel, the simplest of all being to add wooden chairs to a stainless-steel kitchen, or vice versa. This will soften the ambience of a kitchen made entirely from one material, making it both more visually exciting and more comfortable to live with. Equally simple would be to add stainless-steel handles or solid wood knobs. Alternatively, you could add metal appliances and accessories refrigerators, dishwashers, even toasters, or lemon squeezers.

LEFT, ABOVE AND
BELOW This kitchen
offers a gorgeous mix
of old and new in pretty
colors that are eye-
catching, but not over
the top. The blue-and-
white tiles make a
marvelous backdrop to
a set of patterned ceramic
containers and a modern
(albeit classically detailed)
stove. The marble-topped
breakfast table is an
antique find, while the
pink chair is a modern re-
edition of a classic Arne
Jacobsen design. Overall,
the look is light and
feminine, but the kitchen
is practical as well as
good-looking.

RIGHT AND OPPOSITE
A modern range makes an
efficient addition to a
global-style kitchen. The
turquoise tiles and
distinctive star-lantern
introduce a Moorish feel,
but there's an eclectic
atmosphere overall, with
Chinese silk tea cozies
and door knobs from India
and Africa. If you wish to
emulate this look, it is
possible to buy modern
tiles in these vivid colors,
and it would be easy (and
not too expensive) for a
carpenter to make solid,
simple cabinets such as
these. All you need to do
is splash on a coat of
paint and enjoy adding
quirky accessories.

gLORIOUS COLOR

It's all too easy to see antiques as a collection of boring brown furniture.
But there are a wealth of ways in which to inject luscious color by
using a mix of old and new. And the kitchen is ideal for this treatment:
in living rooms, bedrooms, and bathrooms, you may want calm, glamour
or relaxation, but in the kitchen you can afford a little over-the-top
exuberance and uninhibited fun.

Going global is one means of interpreting this look, choosing a fusion
of ethnic pieces to create a fun and funky feel. One item may provide
a focal point, such as a Moroccan star lantern, a painted Oriental screen,
or a Gujerati embroidered door-hanging. Or you may prefer to combine
a host of items from around the world—Chinese silk tea cozies, Mexican
glassware, salvaged French blue-and-white tiles—for an eclectic mix
that is rich, exotic, and unusual.

An alternative is to find retro-style pieces in vivid, unsubtle color combinations, from Jacobsenesque dining chairs in bubblegum pink to food containers in pretty pastels. Or simply choose modern items, from table linen to china, tiles to lighting, that feature bold, bright shades, mixing them with old tables, chairs, and cupboards. If all else fails, you can always add some intensely colored bowls and plates, a vivid free-standing lamp, or some homemade artwork, and paint bland built-in cabinets in strong, attractive colors.

OPPOSITE A combination of egg-yolk yellow walls and woodwork painted cobalt blue provides the background for a kitchen in which colors are strong and bright. The old cupboard, filing cabinet, chairs, and table are all in distressed brown wood, but the dishes are the most eye-catching element. It is a mix of handmade pieces by eminent ceramicist Rupert Spira, and inexpensive pieces from chain stores.

LEFT, ABOVE A collection of old Indian lassi cups makes an unusual display as well as providing handy storage for kitchen utensils.

LEFT, BELOW This huge sink and elegant faucet were both found in salvage yards; their utilitarian good looks make a good foil for kitsch Oriental ceramics and a child's painting.

RIGHT 1950s-meets-Oriental in this informal dining area. The chairs and table have the characteristic splayed, tapering legs of 1950s design, while the coolie shade of the lamp on the right, combined with the antique screen and chest, adds a Chinese note to this quirky mix.

LEFT In this open-plan 1970s house, the dining table and chairs, 1950s designs by Charles and Ray Eames, double as an occasional workspace. Their plastic and metal finish is in perfect harmony with the modern white kitchen in the background, while a wooden floor, minimal accessories, and bare window provide an ideal setting for the look.

ABOVE This 1960s penthouse apartment was refitted in the 1990s. The kitchen itself couldn't be more modern, with plain white and glass-fronted units and stainless steel. The Tulip dining set, however, is by Eero Saarinen and dates from 1957 and, although the table's teak top and the chocolate-colored

corduroy seats of the chairs are very much of their time, the combination is wonderfully harmonious and effective.

FAR RIGHT, ABOVE A mid-century table and a barely-there wire chair designed by Harry Bertoia are fabulously in keeping with the minimal aesthetic of this modern kitchen.

FAR RIGHT, BELOW The bold black outlines of a set of Arne Jacobsen 3107 dining chairs are a focal point in this room, their color picked up by a plate on display, a wire vase, and a picture frame. White walls and sisal matting are a natural foil to this graphic look, while a pair of minimal shelves allow for interesting displays of a few carefully chosen modern pieces.

mid-century modern

There's something very distinctive about furniture designed in the middle of the twentieth century. Not only does it possess classic good looks and timeless appeal, but it mixes effortlessly with modern architecture and furnishings, never looking frumpy or outdated but always fresh and inspiring. A marvelous place to incorporate such mid-century designer pieces in your home is in the kitchen or dining area.

Sadly, it's no longer possible to come across such furniture in yard sales, dumpsters, or house clearances—its popularity means that prices are high, but you can still source it through specialized dealers or at auctions. Alternatively, several firms still continue to manufacture pieces to the original designs, while others produce close copies that, to the non-purist, are just as attractive.

To make sure this particular mix of old and new really looks its best, get rid of clutter and reduce accessories to a minimum. The lines of these pieces are pure and pared down, and you should make sure they can be seen without unnecessary distraction. Walls painted in white, off-white, taupe, stone, or beige provide a subtle backdrop, as do

bare wooden floors and windows. The square, regular shapes of a modern kitchen perfectly complement mid-century furniture, particularly if you pay attention to details such as handles and faucets. Lighting should be similarly well thought out; modern recessed spotlights are ideal for this sort of scheme, throwing light exactly where required without drawing attention to themselves. Alternatively, a simple shade, either antique or modern, works well hung low over a dining table.

Even the most minimal and hi-tech of contemporary kitchens can look wonderful combined with mid-century furnishings—sleek stainless-steel or lacquered white cabinets work beautifully with curving plastic, wood, or metal. Steer clear of paneled cupboards with fussy detailing or anything that look remotely rustic—this is a forward-looking, urban style. Accessories, too, such as storage jars, pots and pans, utensils, and gadgets, should be selected for their clean lines and clarity of form, in materials such as stainless steel, glass, and chrome. If anything hits the wrong note, the solution is simple—hide it in a cupboard and firmly close the door.

OPPOSITE, ABOVE LEFT
An Eames chair integrates seamlessly into a modern stainless-steel kitchen. Its duck's-egg blue coloring picks up the shades of the glass and ceramics displayed on the retro shelving behind.

OPPOSITE, BELOW LEFT
A built-in kitchen in glossy white and stainless steel is home to an array of classic gadgets and these attractive and unusual retro-style chairs.

OPPOSITE, RIGHT, ABOVE AND BELOW Mid-century chairs mix happily with a robust antique table and a modern, leather-covered side cube.

ABOVE Paul Goldman designed these Cherner chairs in 1957. Grouped around a matching dining table, they make a striking centerpiece in an up-to-date kitchen with wooden floors and a stainless-steel splashback.

RIGHT A classic Noguchi paper lantern hovers above a dining table with integrated candle holders designed by an architectural practice called, appropriately enough, The Moderns. The plywood and metal Arne Jacobsen chairs perfectly complement the materials used elsewhere in the room.

cooking & eating: GETTING IT RIGHT

* Combine and contrast textures for a feel that is inviting and individual: smooth, shiny stainless steel against rough, bare brickwork, or grained wood against soft cotton upholstery, for example.

* Provide plenty of storage—but not necessarily in the form of built-in modern cabinets. Old hutches, cupboards, butchers' blocks, and open shelves are all great additions to the mix.

* Modern kitchens tend to be very square and hard-edged. If this look doesn't suit you, add furniture with curvy outlines (such as old Paris café chairs) or items that are softer and more giving—perhaps an antique Turkish kilim under a dining table, or a pair of pretty 1950s curtains.

* Create straightforward contrasts between old and new by choosing objects that are well defined and simple in style. If a piece combines more than one style in itself, it will only create visual clutter and detract from the overall look.

* Keep walls and floors plain, and minimize clutter, so that both antique and modern pieces—such as an English oak dining table combined with a set of 1950s Scandinavian chairs —are shown at their best.

* It's best to choose modern appliances that work efficiently—stoves, dishwashers, exhaust fans and so on—and mix them with older accessories, or hide them behind specially made cabinet doors.

* Be disciplined when it comes to open shelves and work surfaces. Having too many small items on display is never as effective as a few carefully chosen pieces. One huge antique wooden bowl full of fruit will have much more impact than lots of smaller bits and pieces.

* Remember that there are now plenty of companies that specialize in modern accessories in classic retro designs—juicers, blenders, and toasters, to name but a few. Use them to inject instant old-and-new style.

* Bear in mind that the heights of old and new chairs and dining tables may not match up—always take measurements carefully before you rush into making a purchase.

* Old cabinets and hutches can sometimes be massively improved by changing the knobs or handles, or by replacing cracked or warped door panels with fabric, chicken wire, or sandblasted or etched glass.

sLeepInG

The bedroom is a private space, which allows you to be more creative in your approach to its decoration. It's the perfect home for your treasured old and new pieces, but for a harmonious mix, keep things plain and unassuming, and restrict yourself to just one or two dramatic flourishes. Don't cram lots of accessories into the room—clutter is not restful or relaxing.

THIS PAGE AND OPPOSITE Sheer curtains of a loose metallic weave diffuse the natural light as it falls upon a disparate collection of pieces that coexist in perfect harmony. The antique mahogany bed, set off by pale lilac walls, highlights the very different texture and color of a sleek white-leather Mies van der Rohe chair. However, the two items have in common a curvaceous opulence that is set off by the luxurious fur throw and rug.

LEFT What could be more inviting than layers of white bed linen? Here, they have been combined with an old iron bed with pretty detailing. The effect is spare and utilitarian but is ultimately calming and relaxing.

RIGHT In another plain and simple bedroom, an old chair sits next to a divan, acting as an impromptu bedside table. The white bed linen emphasizes the pared-down purity of the space.

LEFT This plain modern divan is adorned with an old American patchwork quilt in muted pinks. Next to the bed, a couple of old trunks take the place of a bedside table. Over the bed, a large modern painting by American artist Peter Zangrillo acts as an unusual headboard.

RIGHT A good lamp is essential for bedtime reading. This antique hinged-arm version is beautifully simple yet eminently functional.

pure & simple

For a bedroom that is a relaxed, calming space in which to refresh the senses, aim to create an atmosphere of tranquil simplicity. Essential to this look is a room that is airy rather than cramped, spacious rather than cluttered. Even in the smallest of bedrooms, you can make sure this is the case by hiding away any inessentials, leaving just the key pieces: a bed, a side table, lamp, mirror, closet, and perhaps a chair and one or two accessories. A plain floor is best, either scrubbed wood, natural matting, or plain carpet with, if necessary, a single rug beside the bed. Walls, too, should be plain and pale, increasing the feeling of spaciousness and light. A painting or two will add a personal touch, but avoid any garish colors or heavy frames.

The bed is, of course, the key item. A modern divan is nicely understated, and many have the benefit of a large storage drawer underneath; an antique bed will be prettier, if perhaps not quite so practical. Victorian iron beds, for example, are lovely, and provide a welcome note of decorative detail in a room that is very pared down.

The other essentials for comfort are textiles. Try not to obscure light at the windows, keeping curtains and drapes as simple as possible and avoiding fussy pleating and draping, valances and tiebacks. Voile makes

LEFT When you use patterned fabrics in this type of scheme, make sure they're minimal in style. These basic striped mattress tickings are absolutely ideal.

ABOVE A collection of black-and-white family photographs are hung on a clothesline, and look all the better for this unpretentious treatment.

RIGHT A four-poster doesn't have to be an imposing affair. This one has been made from scaffolding poles, making an industrial contrast to the chintz bedspread.

gorgeous, inexpensive curtains, while cotton (perhaps with a very small pattern) or ticking can be made into a pair of simple gathered drapes. Wooden colonial-style shutters or a wooden Venetian blind are two simple alternatives.

On the bed, choose white bed linen with the most delicate of trimmings. Then either layer white on white with duvet covers, blankets, and throws, or seek antique textiles that have subtle patterning, either patchwork quilts, satin-edged blankets, floral bedcovers, or crochet throws. Make sure there is a simple but practical bedside table to hold a book, a clock, and a small vase of flowers. The finishing touches are a directional bedside lamp and dimmable general lighting to create a soft and restful atmosphere.

LEFT This antique French bed is grand in style, but its grandeur is offset by plain walls and extra-wide wooden floorboards. Colored lampshades and soft pashmina throws add to the feeling of luxury.

RIGHT Vintage florals are the ultimate in femininity. Use them as the basis for a simple and pretty guest bedroom. Here, a dark wooden bedstead has been painted a chalky white and teamed with a chintz bedspread. The finishing touch is an armful of hydrangeas in an old enamel bucket.

BELOW Luscious textiles, such as these Chinese silk pillows, add a note of opulence and glamour to a simple, feminine bedroom.

uLtrafeminine bedrooms

Fashions may be becoming more modern and minimal, pared down, and practical, but there'll always be a part of most women that can't resist the opulence of an ultrafeminine bedroom. This is a real boudoir, a sanctuary offering escape from the stresses and realities of the outside world, a haven that possesses comfort and glamour in equal measures.

Old and new combine perfectly in this type of bedroom. It is, for example, the ideal setting for a magnificent antique bed, a one-off investment purchase that makes a bold statement and captivates the eye. It could be a four-poster or an old metal bed, or made from intricately carved or prettily painted wood—what's important is that it has a sumptuous, indulgent feel. Add an old chaise longue, an oversized mirror, or a French armoire—all pieces that will contribute to a evocative, romantic atmosphere.

The other major consideration for a boudoir bedroom is the use of textiles. Even a relatively plain bedroom can be transformed by floral fabrics or plenty of patchwork quilts or pashmina throws. The key is not

RIGHT This unusual antique bed takes pride of place in a modern bedroom, its opulence emphasized by simple, plain white bed linen. It's paired with an antique ottoman and dressing table, the latter topped with a Venetian glass mirror—the ideal accessory in an ultrafeminine bedroom. A shocking-pink Indian shawl injects a splash of hot color.

OPPOSITE A carved wooden four-poster dominates a simple bedroom with roughly plastered walls and a wooden floor. It is unquestionably the focal point, and the rest of the furnishings are understated to show it off at its best.

BELOW LEFT An elegant chaise longue is topped with velvet pillows and a gold sari with metallic-thread embroidery. The ultimate in sensuality and glamour.

BELOW RIGHT Piles of plump antique quilts and bedcovers are a pretty addition to this look.

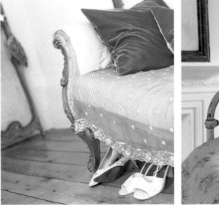

to be restrained: you need layer upon cozy layer to make the room really look the part. Choose pinks, lilacs, soft blues, and glamorous golds and bronzes, and remember that texture is important, too—team shiny Chinese silks with embroidered and beaded Indian pieces and soft, fluffy cashmere, keeping an eye out in antique stores for vintage pieces that can be adapted as throws or pillow covers.

To complete the look, display a generous abundance of accessories. Pile patterned scatter cushions on top of one another; layer quilts, throws, and bedcovers on the ends of beds, even when they are not in use; either hang pretty pictures and ornate mirrors on the walls or prop them on the floor; and, finally, heap an excess of flowers in a large container so that their heady scent floats throughout the room.

LEFT AND OPPOSITE
The undulating form of this elegant, curving screen is underlined by that of the modern chaise longue. Wood-paneled walls and a rug add to the sense of refined luxury.

RIGHT AND BELOW In this masculine bedroom, a carefully considered color scheme beautifully pulls together old (a Bertoia Diamond chair dating from 1952) and new (a pair of Richard Sapper Tizio lamps). Blue and white is a classic combination that invariably looks stylish.

UNDERSTATED eLeGance

For a good night's sleep, we need a comfortable bed and calm surroundings—a muted color scheme, simple furniture, subtle lighting. They all add up to a bedroom that is sophisticated and elegant, where antiques are combined with chic modern pieces to create an atmosphere that promotes rest and relaxation.

To create this look, the emphasis is not placed on one exotic item, but rather on natural combinations of furniture and accessories that blend into one seamless whole. The bed itself could even be relatively ordinary—a divan is fine—but should be dressed with attractive linens with a chic, tailored appearance. Avoid fuss or frills of any kind, and instead think Brooks Brothers suiting, with narrowly striped or hemstitched sheets. Emphasize the sense of luxury by covering the floor with luscious deep-pile rugs, perhaps with a subtle pattern; you could even hang a rug on the wall for a rich and sumptuous effect. Or walls could be paneled with wood veneer, like an upscale gentleman's club.

In general, furnishings should be kept to a minimum, each piece chosen for its quality of materials and manufacture. Secondhand finds are unlikely to make the grade, but classic designer pieces are ideal, with the

LEFT This tranquil bedroom bathed in light adopts a multicultural approach. Pieces collected by the owner on her travels, all in neutral colors and made to high standards, have been carefully put together to create an eclectic yet harmonious whole.

ABOVE The taupe and ivory color scheme in this plush and luxurious bedroom creates a mood of calm contemplation. The oversized headboard in beige linen, teamed with layers of bed linen in carefully coordinating colors, make an ordinary divan look impressive, while the cowhide-covered ottoman adds a lighthearted touch. The swing-arm reading lamps attached to the wall on each side of the bed are attractive and useful—an essential element in this type of scheme.

emphasis on function as well as aesthetics. A bedside table, a chair or chaise longue, perhaps a screen to disguise a dressing area, are all that's needed—they could be old or new, American, European, or Far Eastern, as long as they demonstrate fine forms and good workmanship.

Lighting is vital to getting this look right. Recessed downlighters set in the ceiling will give general illumination without unwanted glare or dazzle, while for reading in bed a pair of adjustable lamps is best—either sitting at an appropriate height on a bedside table, or attached to the wall behind and to the side of the bed. Modern lamps are ideal for this purpose, and have the sort of sleek, slimline design that fits well with this understated scheme.

Perhaps the most important consideration of all, however, is color. Avoid bright shades in favor of naturals and neutrals: white, taupe, ivory, stone, shell, and so on. They will all emphasize space and light, and result in a calm, considered atmosphere. For a more masculine approach, choose shades of gray, from dove to charcoal, and navy, or even deep reds and greens, resulting in a warm and intimate space that is nevertheless refined, dignified, and tasteful.

sLeepiNg: GETTING IT RIGHT

* Avoid bedroom clutter by investing in spacious closets, armoires, and chests of drawers. These could be modern and built-in, with invisible push-touch hinges, or antique versions for a more dramatic and individual statement.

* The bed should be the focal point of the room. If you can afford a beautiful antique style, keep the linen simple and understated, so the bed's design can really stand out. If it's a plain modern divan, layer throws, quilts, and pillows for a more luxurious effect.

* Clever color schemes can pull the whole look together, uniting antique and modern pieces seamlessly. Generally, pale colors such as ivory and taupe are calming and restful, but stronger colors can sometimes be more cozy and inviting. If you have a wonderful bed, you may wish to paint just the wall behind the bed to draw attention to it.

* Keep flooring neutral to provide a plain backdrop that shows off furniture with interesting shapes and colors to its best advantage.

* A bedside rug is wonderfully comforting underfoot. Make sure it is plain or features a subtle pattern that doesn't detract from other furnishings.

* Even if you invest in a wonderful antique bed, you should always buy a good-quality new mattress. We spend an average of twenty-five years of our lives in bed, so it's worth making sure it's not lumpy, too hard, or too soft.

* Choose furniture that works together by virtue of color, shape, or material. The less fussy the decoration and the cleaner the lines, the more likely that old and new pieces will harmonize well.

* Dimmable lights are a good idea for overall illumination. Recessed downlighters in the ceiling will work with an old-and-new scheme because they don't draw any attention to themselves.

* Accessories can provide pretty touches in a bedroom scheme, from enamel pitchers to chintz-printed bowls, an old sari used as a bedcover to a Venetian-glass mirror, an African stool to a tailor's dummy. Just make sure you don't cram the room with too much stuff. Choose pieces that contribute to the overall look and provide a balance with other furnishings.

* Whether it's a sleek, modern halogen light or a 1930s chrome version, always provide an adjustable bedside lamp for easy reading.

Bathing

A bathroom should be an oasis—an intimate place for contemplation, pampering, and relaxation. Here, a combination of old and new gives a sense of luxury and individuality that will provide endless pleasure. Sharp juxtapositions such as 21st-century faucets with a 19th-century roll-top bathtub create a sense of drama, while subtler details provide pause for thought and a chance to unwind in idyllic surroundings.

THIS PAGE AND OPPOSITE
The sharp, square outline of this huge tub, covered in mosaic tiles (in an appropriate shade of turquoise), is very modern. The effect is tempered by the addition of a pair of antique cross-head faucets and, in the background, a cast-iron column radiator. The gently worn patina of these old pieces softens the room and enriches it with a sense of timeless comfort.

LEFT AND OPPOSITE This ultrasimple bathroom is also ultra-tranquil, thanks to the elegant sparsity of its furnishings. An old-fashioned roll-top bathtub contrasts marvelously with avant-garde Philippe Starck faucets and a wide basin with an exposed chrome drain. An expanse of parquet flooring sets everything off beautifully, and the sense of space is emphasized by a huge mirror—a great trick in any room if you want to increase the light and sense of space.

RIGHT The pair of carvings placed symmetrically in a triangular chimneybreast are the focal point of this fashion designer's bathroom. The plain wall provides an understated backdrop for the more ornate fireplace and traditional faucets.

totaL tranquiLity

For a bathroom that's a haven of tranquility and an oasis of calm, there's no better style than one that is pared down to the bare essentials. With no clutter to distract you from a long hot soak with essential oils and a candle, this is a room guaranteed to refresh and revive.

Central to this look is a really comfortable bathtub—if possible one that is slightly larger than average and, maybe, if you're very lucky, a free-standing one. An Edwardian roll-top version with claw feet is ideal, though they're not as easy to come by now as they once were. Some companies, however, make high-quality reproductions that look just as attractive as the originals. An ordinary built-in bathtub can be made more attractive with the addition of an interesting side panel, perhaps in varnished or painted marine plywood, or covered with tiny mosaic tiles.

RIGHT As minimal as can be, this bathtub is a rectangular box sunk deep into the floor of an intimate side room. Tiny mosaic tiles and a stone wall provide plenty of visual interest, however.

LEFT A massive iroko wood screen separates a bathroom from the master bedroom and acts as a headboard for the bed. The rich tones of the wood provide a warm contrast to the pale-blue mosaic tiles that line the bathing area beyond.

RIGHT, ABOVE White-on-white ceramic tiling creates a peaceful bathroom that is simple, clean, and serene.

RIGHT, BELOW, LEFT TO RIGHT Plain accessories are best for this type of scheme; a tiled room is the ultimate in minimal showering.

OPPOSITE An expanse of frosted glass creates an ethereal effect that is emphasized by pale colors and clean lines. Fluffy white towels are a welcome addition to this tranquil bathroom, adding a cozy, tactile touch.

For an intriguing juxtaposition of old and new, combine an old bathtub or washbasin with minimal, ultramodern faucets and shower attachments. You could also offset a sleek new sink by setting it against a roughly plastered wall, or hang an old Venetian-glass or wood-framed mirror above a thoroughly modern glass basin. While it's best to keep other furnishings to a minimum in a bathroom, if the space is available you may wish to add an antique chest or cabinet for storing towels and toiletries, or a chair or stool on which to place discarded clothes, books, and the like.

Most important of all, use colors that are muted, subtle, and sophisticated. One wall painted turquoise or deep red will look wonderfully effective, as will wood paneling and one or two pieces of freestanding furniture made from dark wood, but the overall effect should be light and airy, to create as peaceful an atmosphere as you possibly can.

opulent inDulGence

If you want a bathroom that makes a statement—a dramatic space in which you'll feel invigorated and inspired—aim to create a high-impact look that mixes old and new with imagination and flair, resulting in drop-dead gorgeousness and over-the-top glamour.

The secret to achieving this wow factor is usually one extraordinary item, whether it's an incredible view, an unusual tub or an impressive mirror. Specialists in antique sanitaryware sometimes have amazing old bathtubs, huge shower heads, and oversized, patterned basins—but they don't come cheap. A less expensive alternative is to use plain modern fixtures and combine them with strong paint colors and interesting free-standing pieces, such as chairs, side tables, chests, or cabinets.

TOP, LEFT AND CENTRE Antique copper bathtubs, with their rich color and opulent curves, are the perfect focal point for an old-and-new bathroom.

TOP RIGHT A series of framed black-and-white architectural prints covers the walls of this bathroom, creating the sort of traditional "print-room" effect more usually encountered in a living or dining room. This is a clever way to jazz up a boring bathroom (you could even used framed photocopies), although it would not be wise to put expensive artworks in a damp environment.

RIGHT The many and varied elements of this bathroom are elaborate and dramatic, but because they share a similar design style, the effect is opulent rather than discordant.

LEFT The impact of this bathroom is generated, primarily, by its jaw-dropping view. However, the lovely antique bathtub and shower fixture come a close second, contrasting wonderfully with the ultramodern floor-to-ceiling windows.

RIGHT This impressively intricate brass faucet-and-shower fixture is rendered more dramatic by the plainness of its original tiled background.

Another way of making a statement without going to huge expense is to use colored or patterned tiles on the floor or the walls. These could be richly colored Moroccan tiles, delicate mosaics, or antique Victorian examples found at a salvage yard.

Because this look is intended to be ornate and sumptuous, look for pieces with elaborate, decorative shapes and forms—bring on the gilt, the carving, the rich embellishments. For a unified look, however, keep to a coherent color scheme, and make sure that your furnishings either all date from the same period or show a similar decorative intent.

ABOVE This bright and airy city bathroom has a dash of glamour in the shape of a lovely antique giltwood mirror hung above the washbasin. Elsewhere, the fixtures are plain and simple.

RIGHT An indulgent bathroom need not be full of showy furnishings—here, sophisticated lighting, a large silver-colored mirror, and a sleek wall of custom-made cabinets topped with glass make it a delightfully luxurious space in which to unwind.

ABOVE, LEFT AND RIGHT Unusual free-standing furniture can add plenty of personality to a bathroom.

LEFT Interesting tilework, a lovely old sink, and a shelf unit that was once a shop display add up to a bathroom with endless character.

OPPOSITE Plain walls and flooring provide the perfect backdrop for a large Victorian tub, a wrought-iron trolley, and a pretty Venetian-glass mirror that all possess a sense of opulence.

FAR LEFT Painted beams and wooden walls give this bathroom a simple, spare country feel that is emphasized by the large square tub and ceramic-tiled floor.

LEFT Old oak beams and painted wooden boards are appealingly down-to-earth. The tiled sink area adds a dash of color and pattern.

BELOW LEFT Old wood and bright stripes are a bold combination. The dramatic paintwork draws attention from the bland modern toilet.

BELOW RIGHT An old punched-metal pail has been converted into an unusual but actually very efficient washbasin. The ultramodern faucet teamed with it provides an unexpected and intriguing contrast.

RURaL RetReat

The country-style bathroom is simple and functional, uncomplicated and unpretentious, with a leisurely yet slightly utilitarian feel. It offers a welcome retreat from modern life—somewhere to relax and unwind.

Natural materials are at the heart of this look, and most essential of all is wood. If you are lucky enough to have a bathroom with a beamed ceiling, leave the wood bare or paint it white, duck's-egg blue or sunny yellow. Tongue-and-groove wall paneling adds a country flavor to any room while providing a durable and practical wall covering, especially when coated with paint specially formulated for bathrooms. Stripped floorboards will also strike the right note, although in a colder climate you might want to add warm rag rugs or cotton runners underfoot. Accessories in other unassuming materials, such as enameled buckets,

ABOVE In a newly converted attic bathroom, an antique dresser and rustic stool have been placed below a window to make the most of natural light. The country feel of this room arises from the exposed beams and plentiful use of stripped wood.

LEFT The tongue-and-groove paneling on the walls of this light and airy bathroom has been painted a pretty nautical blue. The "telephone" shower attachment adds a traditional touch.

straw or wicker baskets, and handpainted ceramic tiles will help to create an effect of simple and uncontrived rusticity.

The idea of going back to nature is an appealing one, but not many of us could do without modern comforts. In a country-style bathroom, it's essential to strike a balance between practicality and prettiness. Choose modern fixtures such as reproduction roll-top bathtubs or chunky faucets that work well while possessing old-fashioned good looks. Carefully chosen power showers, heated towel rods, and good lighting all have their place in a rural retreat, making for a bathroom that's enjoyably easy to spend time in—heartwarming, welcoming, and homey.

ABOVE A huge built-in closet that covers an entire wall holds all sorts of essential bathroom paraphernalia that is best kept out of sight. The warmth of the natural wood adds greatly to the room's calm and cozy atmosphere.

RIGHT Spacious bathrooms always have a peaceful feel, and this country-style interior is particularly pleasant, with lots of natural light. The runners on the floor provide warmth underfoot without being fussy.

bathing: GETTING IT RIGHT

* Adding old freestanding pieces (chairs, chests, even a tub) is a good way to break out of the boring built-in mold. Do leave as much floor area as possible clear, however, in order to create a spacious, airy feel—remember that the spaces between the furnishings are just as important as the furnishings themselves.

* If you are on a budget, install inexpensive, plain white modern sanitaryware. Look out for interesting pieces of freestanding furniture and pretty accessories in flea markets and secondhand stores that will stand out against the modern fixtures and make more of an impact.

* If necessary, you can have old bathtubs re-enameled so that their surfaces are clean, new, and pleasant to bathe in.

* When buying old bathroom fixtures, it's important to check that all dimensions will match up with modern plumbing.

* If you are thinking of installing a large reclaimed cast-iron tub, first make sure your floor is strong enough to support the combined weight of the bathtub, the water, and a bather—a substantial load. Check with a structural engineer if in any doubt.

* Use tiles to unify a scheme. With opulent or dramatic antiques, plain white tiles are an ideal background, while with rather less exotic modern fixtures, colored and handpainted tiles (whether old or new) can be used to introduce more atmosphere.

eLements

Antique furniture can sometimes appear heavy and dark—difficult to fit into a contemporary home. However, using pale cotton or canvas slipcovers or cushions, or even simply swathing fabric around a chair, will instantly update a piece and imbue it with an air of lightness and modernity.

furniture

The building blocks of any home, furniture comes in many guises, and a combination of old and new can be both effective and appealing. You may simply wish to add an antique stool to an otherwise contemporary living room, or you may prefer to create an eclectic mix that brings together pieces from different periods in an inspiring way. Either way, carefully chosen chairs and tables, chests and cupboards can underline connections and contrasts between one era and another.

OPPOSITE, LEFT **Lofty glass-paneled doors and a stone floor provide a clean backdrop for a 1970 Rocker chair by Marc Held. Its generous curves offset the linearity of the architecture.**

OPPOSITE, ABOVE RIGHT **A comfortable club chair in burnished leather is perfectly at home in a room with modern stripped floorboards and plain white walls.**

OPPOSITE, BELOW RIGHT **Covering the cushions of this old cane chair in white cotton allows it to fit in well with minimal surroundings, despite its traditional style. The fabric creates a contrast with the chair's carved wooden detailing.**

seating

Chairs are key pieces in the old-and-new look. From a battered leather club chair to a 21st-century steel one, or a bentwood Thonet chair to a 1950s-style dining chair upholstered in zebra skin, these items of furniture are often inexpensive and easy to find, while being simple to move around, to re-upholster or cover, or to accessorize with throws or scatter cushions. It's easy to make an antique chair work in a contemporary room, or a new chair in a period setting.

Sometimes it's the clash of cultures that makes mixing old and new most interesting, and introducing a chair from one period into a home from another can be one of the easiest and quickest ways to achieve this. In an older house, with paneling, ceiling or wall moldings, brickwork, or exposed beams, introduce a very different element in the shape of a Danish mid-twentieth-century chair, a 1960s plastic stool, or a 21st-century clear acrylic chair. The juxtaposition of the two aesthetics will be striking: setting plastic against rough plasterwork or steel against paneling is surprisingly effective. The key to making the look work is to keep other furnishings to a minimum, and avoid garish or distracting

ABOVE LEFT **A roomy antique armchair has been re-upholstered in checked tweed, adding a spin to a timeless design.**

ABOVE RIGHT **A pink pashmina shawl and rose-print pillow bring a very modern sense of relaxation to the square lines of this mid-century armchair.**

RIGHT **A unexpected combination. The lightness of the wire Bertoia chair makes it a versatile choice—it has minimal impact, but possesses great flair.**

patterns or over-complex forms. Trying too hard will only result in confusion, but allow the pieces to speak for themselves and they will interact with their surroundings in the most positive way.

If your home is modern in style, an antique chair can introduce a note of old-fashioned comfort, a dash of opulence, or an element of sophisticated chic. Leather club chairs, buttoned armchairs upholstered in checks or tweed, Louis-style carved wooden chairs, or Victorian cane chairs all have marvelous character and bring a room to life. Such elements will prevent a modern home from becoming bland, while glass-and-steel lofts often benefit from the addition of an unexpected piece that contrasts with their sleek architectural detailing.

Secondhand stores, auctions, and the less expensive antique dealers are all good sources for old chairs. Sometimes they may be a little battered and tired—this may simply add to their appeal, or you may prefer to have them repaired or given a new coat of paint, stain, or varnish. Often the most unpromising piece can blossom into a beauty when it is painted the right color. Reupholstering an old chair also makes a huge difference to its appearance: using a plain, heavy off-white cotton or canvas adds simplicity and allows most pieces to fit into most rooms. Alternatively, you could be daring and choose a bold "statement" fabric that contrasts with a more traditional shape in an exciting and dynamic way. Slipcovers may be a less expensive option.

BELOW LEFT Marco Zanuso's Lady armchair looks remarkably modern despite dating back to 1951. Here, its streamlined shape works well in a light-filled contemporary interior that reveals a passion for mid-century styling.

BELOW RIGHT A modern dining table harmonizes perfectly with a set of Saarinen dining chairs. The pieces have in common slender, pared-down forms and simple surfaces.

RIGHT A wooden sculpture, a Brancusi-inspired stool, and a plywood chair by Alvar Aalto make for a striking combination of different shapes and periods.

TOP Mies van der Rohe's Barcelona chair, designed in 1929, is now a modern classic.

ABOVE An Ernest Race Antelope chair, designed in 1951 for the Festival of Britain, makes a bold statement in a modern home.

ABOVE RIGHT Verner Panton's S chair looks positively futuristic, even in a contemporary interior.

RIGHT Simple lines and a pared-down form mean that this Eames chair sits naturally in a contemporary living room.

FAR RIGHT This Robin Day chair has the simple square lines and clean-cut feel that work well in a minimal modern interior.

LEFT At first glance, these chairs appear dissimilar, but in fact their square outlines and firm upholstery mean they have a lot in common. Of course, they still look very different, but these stylistic echoes—even though their designs are centuries apart—means that the pairing creates a harmonious contrast, rather than an uneasy clash.

RIGHT In this light, bright room, a mix of seating creates a prettily informal dining area. Though the chairs (and bench) may represent a wide variety of styles, they share a visual coherence—all are simple to the point of being rustic, without ornamentation of any kind. It helps that the walls and floor, and even the rug and curtains, have been kept deliberately plain, so as not to provide any added distraction.

Bear in mind that old chairs can be found in the most unusual places, from dumpsters to yard sales, outdoor furniture outlets to architectural antique companies. Department stores can provide straightforward modern pieces, or you can go to a specialist for a modern-classic designer chair that blows your bank balance. An interesting chair, of whatever type or style, can single-handedly create an impressive old-and-new look that will set the tone for the rest of your scheme.

LEFT AND FAR LEFT These old folding church chairs in dark wood have a timeless solidity and dignity. They are guaranteed to add depth and character to any room as well as providing useful additional seating.

RIGHT AND OPPOSITE Old outdoor seating works particularly well when it is used indoors. Repainting it adds a certain sophistication, so it doesn't look too out of place next to conventional furnishings.

LEFT The rich carving of this ancient chest provides a strong contrast with the simply framed contemporary photos displayed above it.

ABOVE Office furniture can often be adapted in an attractive and ingenious fashion for home use. Here, the narrow drawers of an old-fashioned wooden architect's chest are useful for storing papers and drawings, and would look good in both a formal or informal setting.

RIGHT The mix of styles in this home office is unobtrusive, because each item of furniture possesses a pleasing simplicity. The old school lockers provide storage for files, computer disks and the like. The lack of clutter and the clean white floor and walls means the overall effect is quirky, not junky.

BELOW RIGHT Some items display such pleasing evidence of wear and tear that it would be a shame to conceal it. With smooth new walls as a backdrop, this old filing cabinet, for example, has a patina of age that is beguilingly tactile.

armoires, chests, & other storage

Every home needs plenty of storage, and a combination of old and new pieces is a clever way in which to blend practicality with aesthetic appeal. Whether in a living room or bedroom, the kitchen or bathroom, a hall or a home office, chests, cabinets, hutches, armoires, and sideboards, both antique or modern, can play a useful role in daily life while also making an invaluable contribution to your decorating scheme.

An immediate way of adding interest to a modern home is to provide a bold feature in the form of an oversized period storage piece. It may be carved or painted, or possess an imposing, scrolling outline—a Renaissance chest, for example, or a 19th-century Italian armoire, an Indian cupboard, a lacquered Oriental cabinet, or a decorative French bureau would all create an impact when set against plain painted walls, bare brickwork, exposed concrete, or metal beams. Equally, they will provide space for all sorts of storage, from wine glasses to towels, drinks to office equipment. Statement pieces such as this tend to be inherited (if you're very lucky) or found at the grander antique stores and auction houses. Less imposing (and less expensive) pieces, however, can also enrich a contemporary room,

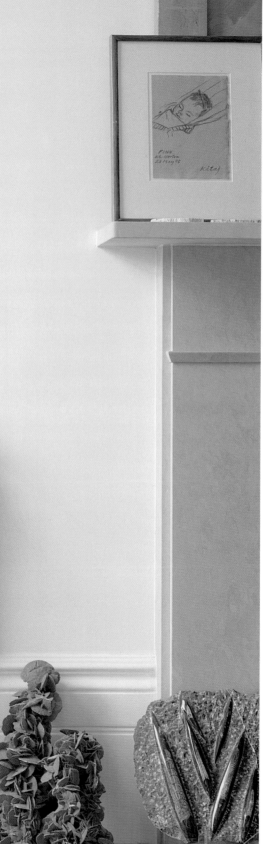

LEFT In an airy modern room, the beautiful grain of an old wooden map chest adds character and individuality. Its large surface also offers the opportunity to create attractive displays.

OPPOSITE, ABOVE LEFT Wall-hung cupboards are a useful way of tucking clutter out of sight. Country-style pieces such as this one are relatively easy to come by.

OPPOSITE, BELOW LEFT Distressed paintwork adds to the character of old wooden pieces.

OPPOSITE, RIGHT This fabulous mirrored armoire has moved from the bedroom to the kitchen, and now acts as a beautiful and unusual food cabinet.

BELOW Muted colors provide a visual link between the old-and-new styles of this cabinet and nearby furnishings.

albeit in a more understated way: country-style hutches, utilitarian filing cabinets, or simple cedar chests, for example, can harmonize nicely with more modern pieces. Such items can sometimes be picked up in house and office clearance sales or secondhand stores relatively easily and tend not to be too expensive, particularly if they need a little renovation in the form of sanding or painting.

In a period home, it's also possible to combine old and new by introducing brand-new storage pieces. Elaborate ceiling molding, baseboards, and paneling can be offset with plain, pared-down cabinets in wood veneer or metal, their sleek surfaces contrasting quietly with the decorative nature of their surroundings. A modern designer sideboard

ABOVE Sometimes simply choosing the right paint color can result in the most creative contrasts between old and new. Here, the color and patina of a recently painted wall superbly offsets those of the 1960s cupboard in front of it.

LEFT Dramatic lighting showcases this antique Chinese scholar's desk. Setting it within a modern brushed-glass screen makes it a focal point in a minimal loft.

could easily become the focal point of a Federal dining room, for example, while a minimal Scandinavian chest of drawers would work in a bedroom with a Shaker four-poster bed. From the most inexpensive chain stores to chic boutiques offering the very latest European designs, keep your eyes open for storage items that will work well in your home. If designer pieces are usually out of your price range, bear in mind that some stores have regular end-of-line sales offering substantial discounts, and it's also well worth checking the Internet for bargains.

An imaginative approach always reaps rewards. After all, at the heart of the old-and-new look is a willingness to embrace experimentation and the unexpected. So, a 1940s polished-steel office filing cabinet would be a quirky place to store shampoo, soap, and other essentials in a bathroom, while a carved wooden armoire could double as a fabulous cocktail cabinet in the living room; a carved oak coffer might hold umbrellas and boots in the hall, or a Tibetan cabinet could conceal a collection of shoes in a spare bedroom. Old pieces can often be adapted to modern uses (although it's unwise to alter valuable antiques of any type)—drill a small hole in the back of an old hutch, for example, and you can pass an electric cord through to a socket, allowing it to house a television, video recorder, or hi-fi system. If necessary, you can even add extra shelving on which to store DVDs, videos, or compact disks.

Sometimes, no adaptation is required. You can easily make a guest room that doubles as a home office appear more welcoming by concealing files, stationery, or even computer equipment inside an antique wooden armoire or cabinet. Failing that, stack them on simple shelves, which can then be concealed by hanging an antique curtain or a length of vintage fabric in front.

ABOVE AND LEFT **Retro pieces, especially those dating from the 1950s, have a distinctive style that gives them great character. They tend to be without paneling, carving, or elaborate outlines, and instead feature tapering legs, plain doors, and a lean, long, low outline that instantly indicates their origin. Attractive items of furniture in their own right, with plenty of personality, they also offer ideal storage for narrow rooms and small spaces, and as an added bonus often provide a great surface for displaying lamps, vases, bowls, or other objects.**

Left A lovely old oak refectory table is given all the more impact by its juxtaposition with a set of classic 3107 dining chairs designed by Arne Jacobsen in 1955.

Above This curvy metal side table may be old, but it has been used in an appealingly modern way, set below a dramatic painting, whose curves echo its form, and a row of crucifixes, to create a theatrical display.

Opposite, Above Left A new wooden dining table is surrounded by old-fashioned rush-seated chairs in front of a Victorian fireplace to create a relaxed dining room.

Opposite, Above Right In an almost-empty room, a low modern table offers the perfect surface for a display of antique Oriental artifacts.

Opposite, Below Right This simple old console table, painted soft white, is an understated piece that harmonizes perfectly with modern side chairs and the airy, pared-down aesthetic of a contemporary living room.

taBles

One of the most exciting opportunities for unusual juxtapositions of old and new is offered by a dining table and its surrounding chairs. A pleasing effect can be gained by contrasting the strength and solidity of a wooden table with a scoured and scrubbed surface with new chairs in smooth plywood, shiny plastic, or sleek steel. Alternatively, combine a chic modern table with old chairs. This look will be even more effective if the chairs don't match, so you can have fun seeking them out in all sorts of places, from yard sales to secondhand stores and even dumpsters.

Side tables, console tables, bedside tables, and, of course, coffee tables can also be essential elements in this type of scheme. A huge coffee table made from reclaimed railroad ties or an old East Indian door would look fabulous in a minimal modern living room, for example, while a slim, contemporary console table, made from pale wood, metal, or sandblasted glass, would be a neat addition to a traditional hall.

Lighting

If you're looking for just one showstopping piece to bring dramatic contrast to a contemporary room, the answer may be a sparkling chandelier, a spindly 1950s floor lamp, or an oversized 1960s plastic lampshade. Antique lighting makes the perfect accessory to modern furnishings, counterpointing clean lines with ornate or over-the-top details, and cool colors with vivid tones.

THIS PAGE AND OPPOSITE Antique chandeliers (and modern reproductions) possess a unique glamour and attention-grabbing appeal. Their sparkly droplets and twining shapes catch the eye and contrast perfectly with minmal contemporary furnishings and accessories.

glamorous

Planning a lighting scheme is crucial when decorating a home, and functional lighting should be installed before any other elements. However, if you want to add a dash of glorious glamour in the shape of decorative lighting, it's best left until last. This means you can forage around secondhand stores and yard and garage sales, and visit antique dealers until you find the perfect piece to complement your room.

Perhaps the most obvious type of glamorous lighting is the antique chandelier, made from wrought metal and faceted glass drops (designed to maximize sparkle) that are either colored or clear. Chandeliers range in style from extremely ornate to relatively simple and, although some cost a fortune, it is still possible to find examples that aren't too expensive. But there are all sorts of alternatives, too, ranging from traditional metal candelabra that can provide a superb contrast to a contemporary living room, to modern, Moorish-style glass lanterns that would look fabulous over a traditional-style dining table. In general, look for intricate shapes, luxurious materials, and intense colors, and the results won't fail to dazzle and delight.

Retro

Lighting from between the 1930s and the 1970s tends to fall into two design styles: the practical and the decorative. The former will often have adjustable supports or a flexible stem, so that light can easily be directed toward work, a book, or a picture, while the latter come in wild colors and unusual shapes that delight the eye and create a focal point.

When choosing lighting to work in an old-and-new scheme, ask yourself whether you want a piece that is functional or simply looks good. Either way, there are plenty of styles to choose, from sturdy 1930s desk lights that would look wonderful in a home office to spindly 1950s lamps with conical shades and bold, shapely 1960s lights guaranteed to make an impact wherever they are placed.

Well-known pieces by named designers command a premium price, but it's still possible to find retro examples in smaller antique stores (and often secondhand office equipment outlets) that are highly affordable. And, of course, some retro-style pieces are still being made today—colorful, quirky lava lamps and groovy, sparkly mirror balls, for example, can be bought in chain stores, to give your home an unabashed injection of dazzling and eye-catching kitsch.

OPPOSITE, LEFT ABOVE The 1962 Arco lamp by the Castiglioni brothers has become an icon of modern design.

OPPOSITE, LEFT BELOW This utilitarian desk lamp is both useful and attractive, in a quiet and unassuming fashion.

OPPOSITE, RIGHT An early 1950s Italian floor lamp brings character to a minimal dining area.

ABOVE Disco fever comes to a quiet corner of the living room in the form of the ever-popular mirrored ball light.

LEFT A bright-red lava lamp adds a quirky and colorful touch to a living room characterized by clean lines and cool neutrals.

ABOVE AND TOP Retro lighting comes in many different shapes and styles, from the strictly functional to the dramatically decorative. Above, the snaking lines of a 1950s lamp are instantly recognizable, while the elegant white plastic lamp below is Verner Panton's Panthella.

textiLes

Whether in the bedroom or the living room, textiles help to create an atmosphere of comfort and coziness. Vintage textiles, in particular—in the form of curtains, bedspreads, rugs, pillow covers, tablecloths, throws, or wall-hangings—will add a sense of comfort and charm, making even the most modern and minimal homes feel warm and welcoming.

THIS PAGE AND OPPOSITE In the plainest of rooms, a delicately colored and patterned bedspread introduces welcome color and interest. The softness of fabric contrasts beautifully with the hard surfaces of flooring, furniture, and architectural detailing.

fLoraL faBRICS

Using old floral fabrics is a quick way to add prettiness, color, and individuality to a modern room. From delicate sprigs to blowsy blooms, there are patterns suitable for any scheme, in soft pastels or more vivid shades. In living rooms, use them as curtains or upholstery, if you have enough fabric, or make pillows from smaller pieces. In dining rooms, floral fabrics can be used as tablecloths, runners, or napkins, while in bedrooms they can come in the form of pillowcases, bedspreads, or quilts.

CLOCKWISE FROM FAR LEFT Lengths of floral fabric can be used to cover storage boxes or lampshades; Look for lengths of vintage fabric in flea markets and antique stores—you can hang them on your walls or frame them like a painting; Floral fabrics make ideal pillow covers, and look particularly nice placed on a plain white chair—whether painted-wood or upholstered—for contrast; Plenty of companies manufacture beautiful prints such as these, which are taken from archival patterns and are virtually indistinguishable from their antique counterparts; Fabric printed with tiny sprigged flowers on a pale or white background is one of the easiest to use in any room.

OPPOSITE A cozy quilt made from old floral fabric will be the focal point of any bedroom. Quilts look especially appealing on painted wooden or metal beds.

utiLitarian

In a contemporary house with plain white walls and bare floors, or a minimal loft space with steel and glass, there's nothing nicer than adding textiles to warm up the interior. Sometimes, however, pretty chintz fabrics are not quite appropriate, whereas more practical, utilitarian textiles have the right kind of practical good looks.

The plainest of choices for this type of look is antique linen sheets, washed so many times that they're softer than soft, gorgeous to sleep in or even to use as curtains. Old

OPPOSITE Plump pillows and heavy throws in rich jewel colors bring warmth to an understated contemporary interior. The textiles add a homey air that softens the clean lines and cool neutrals.

BELOW LEFT These pillow covers have been made from old linen towels. Their soft colors mix together beautifully.

LEFT Old blankets and throws add character to modern rooms.

TOP A traditional check has been used to give new lease on life to a simple chair seat.

RIGHT Layered plains, checks, and stripes make for a welcoming, eclectic mix. This sofa positively invites you to curl up on it with a good book.

denim, too, aged by years of use, can be made into covers for scatter cushions, seats, or small windows. Thick wool blankets, in muted colors, are warm and welcoming, whether on a bed or thrown over the back of a sofa, and if you can find examples of old knitting or crochet, they will provide the ultimate in homey, traditional comfort.

All sorts of other old fabrics can also be adapted in a similar way, whether bought as lengths in an antique store or found in the form of a pair of curtains at a garage sale. Even old dishtowels, shirts, or blankets can be cut up and stitched back together, for a casual look that softens the edges of a modern room. For this type of old-and-new mix, use plains, stripes, ginghams, and checks in simple, soft colors—nothing too garish or fussy. But you can create beautiful effects by layering one old fabric on top of another, in harmonizing colors, from pale blue to indigo, or sepia to chocolate, adding subtle warmth and delicious texture to even the coolest of modern environments.

abstract

If you want to create an interior that makes a strong statement and is more chic than chintz, then abstract textiles are ideal. They will work anywhere in the home, in the bedroom, the living room, a hall or a dining room; all rooms, in fact, can benefit from their impact and appeal.

In a modern house or apartment, retro fabrics coordinate well with a pared-down, clean-lined feel. Without overwhelming a contemporary scheme, they can inject a note of color and pattern that provides a pleasant balance or interesting contrast. Fabrics from the 1950s are particularly attractive, with their organic patterns and soft secondary colors. Some examples, such as those designed by Lucienne Day for the 1951 Festival of Britain, are hard to come by and now command high prices at auction, but it is possible to find less well-known designs in secondhand stores and yard sales, often in the form of old curtains or dresses that can be made over into pillow covers, napkins, or throws.

There is a wealth of contemporary fabrics available in abstract patterns, in colors that range from neutrals to brights. In a period home they are amazingly effective, counterpointing architectural detailing or antique furniture. Use them as rugs, bedspreads, cushions or curtains, but use them sparingly, as they can be overwhelming in large quantities. Just one or two pieces will enrich a space with drama and definition.

FAR LEFT, ABOVE AND BELOW Modern rugs in 1930s-style abstract patterns will add a sleek, graphic element to a period interior with ornate architectural features.

CENTER, ABOVE AND BELOW 1960s pillow covers in bold abstract patterns and vivid colors provide a counterpoint to the minimal lines of a classic Florence Knoll sofa dating from 1954.

BELOW LEFT The soft colors of this square-printed tablecloth are redolent of typical 1950s style, and provide a lovely background for plain modern china.

OPPOSITE For a unique look with plenty of impact, choose a bedcover printed or woven in retro-style abstracts. Well-defined shapes and strong colors such as these work best in a room that is otherwise understated.

ceramics

Both useful and beautiful, ceramics are the ideal accessory. Whether sleek and modern, or intricate and antique, they add instant personality and warmth, and come in an infinite variety of styles and colors. Fashionable modern pottery is made in strong, simple shapes with one-color glazes, which look wonderful contrasted with the architectural detailing of a traditional home. Old ceramics, on the other hand—floral prints, blue-and-white Delftware, or characterful retro pieces—look particularly effective in a contemporary setting.

THIS PAGE AND OPPOSITE This colorful, mid-20th-century chinaware is plain and workmanlike in style, yet it still makes a wonderful display on a sideboard in a pared-down, modern home, providing warmth, color, and all the pleasure of the old juxtaposed with the new.

OPPOSITE Chintz-printed tea sets are inexpensive and easy to find. They look particularly effective when displayed in a clean-lined modern kitchen.

LEFT A modern unit has been filled with a host of attractive kitchenware, including mismatching but delightfully pretty sets of old dishes.

RIGHT The delicate pattern of an antique coffee set can be glimpsed through the glass door of a modern kitchen cabinet.

BELOW The timeless quality of traditional blue-and-white china allows it to fit into any style of home, whether old or new.

pretty & nostalgic

There's nothing more appealing than a delicate bone-china teacup decorated with a floral pattern in soft pastels. Inexpensive and easy to come by, these old pieces may not be precious antiques, but they have an old-fashioned charm and friendliness of their own. They can be bought in ones and twos and piled up casually as mismatching sets, either to be put into use or simply as an irresistibly pretty display. In a contemporary home, they provide an ideal and unexpected counterpoint to expanses of white-painted wall, wood or stone flooring, and the clean, boxy lines of modern furnishings.

For traditionalists who prefer a simpler look, the alternative is the equally delightful and ever-popular blue-and-white china. Willow-pattern china is probably the best-known, but any secondhand store is likely have some pieces in blue and white, from all sorts of periods and by a range of manufacturers. Choose them for their pretty shapes and coordinated colors, and display them en masse as a fresh, uncontrived addition to a sophisticated contemporary kitchen or dining room.

retro

Retro ceramics, dating from between the 1920s and the 1970s, have a unique style that gives the finishing touch to a characterful contemporary room scheme. Because they tend to be rather plain, they harmonize well with modern decoration, but nevertheless they possess a distinctive character, either in their charmingly organic shapes, incised sgraffito decoration, or unusual colors, which marks them out as a special choice.

While pieces by the important Modernist designers such as Keith Murray would be a rare discovery, there are endless examples of less significant, but hugely attractive retro ceramics to be found in secondhand stores and yard sales. The key is to pick pieces whose shapes and colors work gracefully together, and to display them in a way that doesn't come across as too cluttered or overpowering.

OPPOSITE, TOP LEFT In the kitchen of an industrial-style loft, a set of wooden shelves provides a quiet corner for curvy 1950s ceramics.

OPPOSITE, TOP CENTER AND RIGHT A 1950s cabinet sits beautifully in this modern room and offers an ideal display area for a set of coffee-colored 1960s mosaic ashtrays. They, in turn, complement the 1970s wallpaper that has been framed above them, which repeats their colors and shapes.

ABOVE New York potter Jonathan Adler is inspired by groovy Scandinavian ceramics from the 1960s and 1970s. This collection of his work contrasts nicely with the 1950s-style fireguard and chair.

RIGHT AND OPPOSITE, BELOW These simple pieces are by arch-Modernist Keith Murray, and their elegant, unadorned forms are typical of his influential 1930s style. They make a marvelous display ranged in a line on a long, lean, contemporary wood-and-metal sideboard.

gLassware

The translucency of glass makes it an ideal partner for rooms either old or new: subtle and shimmering, it adds elegance and individuality without overpowering other furnishings. Simple forms and subtle colors can be found in glass from all eras, complementing both antique pieces and modern designs. The exceptions are bold, bright pieces from the 1960s, which have an impact and character all their own, and will provide a stunning counterpoint to a room that is otherwise pale and understated.

THIS PAGE AND OPPOSITE **These pieces have in common simple silhouettes and lovely soft colors. They stand out best against a white background and would work in a pared-down period room or a chic modern setting. Their glossy, hard surfaces would also make a fabulous contrast to textured furnishings such as a velvet-covered sofa, voile curtains, or a shagpile rug.**

RIGHT AND BELOW These bottle vases are wonderful examples of the sheer vivacity and exuberance of much mid-20th-century design. Their clear, jewel shades and simple silhouettes are offset perfectly by plain white surroundings. The Arne Jacobsen Swan chair nearby dates from the same period, but its simple white upholstery means it takes a step out of the limelight and allows the glassware to shine.

OPPOSITE, LEFT, ABOVE AND BELOW These vases in smoky shades are typical of the 1970s. In color, form, and overall aesthetic, they make a superb counterpoint to the detailing of a period room.

OPPOSITE, RIGHT To look its best, colorful mid-20th-century glass needs a plain backdrop. If the surroundings are too busy or bright, the pieces will lose their impact.

RIGHT This modern Italian glass vase has more than a hint of the 1950s in its joyful colors and sinuous curves.

COLOREd

Colored glassware comes in many guises. In an otherwise pale, minimal, and understated interior, it offers a wonderful way to add an infusion of vitality, vivacity, and a touch of flamboyance.

Pieces from the 1970s in smoky shades have made a comeback as a fashionable accessory, but can still be found in secondhand stores or flea markets. While subtle in color, their unusual forms stand out against the clean lines of modern furnishings. Similarly, bold 1960s pieces have a powerful impact in a contemporary home, though they make even more of a statement in a period setting. Glass made on the Italian island of Murano displays gorgeous color combinations and complex patterning. These pieces, expensive and rare, are inevitably a focal point in any interior, and combine well with sophisticated but understated furnishings. Finally, choose contemporary glass to complement a period home. The right color combinations and simple, flowing lines will resonate quietly in an old-fashioned room.

OPPOSITE, LEFT
A line-up of clear antique wine glasses and hurricane lamps, in typically beautiful, simple forms, makes double the impact thanks to the mirror behind. The subtlety of white on white, with transparent glass, is highly appealing.

OPPOSITE, RIGHT ABOVE Cute salt and pepper pots, reminiscent of a 1950s diner, make a charming and unassuming display on a simple, white-painted mantelpiece.

OPPOSITE, RIGHT BELOW These jaunty glasses are not so subtle, especially with their jaunty swizzle sticks; nevertheless, they are great fun and would contrast wittily with a modern interior.

ABOVE LEFT Old wine and water glasses don't necessarily have to match—if they're all made from clear glass and feature similar forms and simple patterning, they will still look wonderful together.

ABOVE RIGHT A modern use for single items of clear old glassware: useful storage for other objects such as flatware.

LEFT This antique demijohn makes an unusual vase for a highly contemporary display of a single oversized allium.

cLeaR

Clear glass is one of the nicest, simplest additions to any home, creating subtle visual pleasure without going to excess. While it may be quiet and still, clear glass can nevertheless possess strong character and offer delightful decorative qualities.

Clear antique glassware may be shaped in clear, strong lines—a straight-sided water glass or a flowing hurricane lamp, for example. Or it may feature delicate fluting or intricate engraving, either representational or abstract. Each type can bring elegance and eclecticism to an avant-garde home or a simple 20th-century interior. A scheme in which intense colors predominate allows clear glass to provide a graceful counterpoint, while in a room decorated with muted neutrals, clear glass is a subtle addition.

Retro-style glass tends to feature a little more decoration, sometimes in the form of quirky, humorous touches. These pieces are lively and likeable, and will enhance a space that is otherwise relatively unadorned. You can pick them up in secondhand stores and yard sales galore—but choose carefully to make sure that what you end up with is not just cheap clutter, but a selection that is both intriguing and interesting.

Resources

Modern furniture and accessories

Anthropologie
375 West Broadway
New York, NY
800-309-2500 for your
nearest store
www.anthropologie.com
Funky furniture and home
furnishings.

B & B Italia USA
150 East 58th Street
New York, NY 10155
800-872-1697
www.bebitalia.it
Modern furniture by
Citterio, Pesce, Scarpa
and others.

Cassina USA Inc.
155 East 56th Street
New York, NY 10022
800-770-3568
www.CassinaUSA.com
Reissues of designer
classics by Mackintosh, Le
Corbusier, Rietveld, Frank
Lloyd Wright and more.

The Conran Shop
Bridgemarket
415 East 59th Street
New York, NY 10022
212-755-9079
Modern home furnishings,
kitchenware, tableware,
and bathroom accessories.

Crate & Barrel
646 N Michigan Avenue
Chicago, IL 60611
800-996-9960
www.crateandbarrel.com
Good-value furniture and
accessories.

Design Within Reach
455 Jackson Street
San Francisco, CA 94111
800-944-2233
www.dwr.com
20th-century design
classics.

**Domus Design
Collection**
181 Madison Avenue
New York, NY 10016
212-685-0800
www.ddcnyc.com
Modern designs by
Pralo, Mari, Dordoni,
and many others.

Full Upright Position
1101 NW Glisan
Portland, OR 97209
800-431-5134
www.fup.com
20th-century classics
by Aalto, Eames, Le
Corbusier, van der
Rohe and more.

Gansevoort Gallery
72 Gansevoort Street
New York, NY 10014
212-633-0555
www.gansevoortgallery.com
Contemporary pieces in
metal, lighting, glass,
furniture, wood, and
ceramics.

**Heywood-Wakefield
Company**
2300 SW 23rd Street
Miami, FL 33145
305-858-4240
www.heywood-
  wakefield.com
Modern and vintage pieces
and fabric selections.

Ikea
1800 East McConnor
Parkway
Schaumburg, IL 60173
800-434-4532
www.ikea.com
Home basics at great
prices.

John Widdicomb
560 Fifth Street NW
Grand Rapids
MI 49504-5208
800-847-9433
www.johnwiddicomb.com
Exclusively designed
furniture by the original
maker.

Knoll
1235 Water Street
East Greenville, PA 18041
877-61-KNOLL
www.knoll.com
Producers of modern
furniture by modern
architects since 1938.

**Louis Poulsen
Lighting**
3260 Meridian Parkway
Ft. Lauderdale, FL 33331
954-349-2525
www.louispoulsen.com
Exclusive collection of
tabletop, ceiling, table, and
floor lighting fixtures.

Modernica
2118 East Seventh Place
Los Angeles, CA 90021
800-665-3839
www.modernica.net
Seating, tables, lighting,
and modular shelving from
mid-century designers.

MOMA Design Store
44 West 53rd Street
New York, NY 10022
800-447-6662
www.momastore.org
Furniture and accessories
by modern designers such
as Starck and Vasa.

**O Group (Eva Zeisel
Designs)**
152 Franklin Street
New York, NY 10013
212-431-5973
www.theorange
  chicken.com
Deals exclusively in Eva
Zeisel's designs.

Pastense
915 Cole Street, Suite 150
San Francisco
CA 94117-4315
415-242-0128
www.pastense.com
Classic diner furnishings,
including booths, tables,
chairs, and stools.

Pottery Barn
P.O. Box 7044
San Francisco
CA 94120-7044
800-922-9934 for your
nearest store
www.potterybarn.com
Everything from furniture to
decoration details, such as
muslin curtains, china,
pillows, and candlesticks.

Retromodern.com
805 Peachtree Street
Atlanta, GA 30308
877-724-0093
www.retromodern.com
Designs for the home from
Alessi, Nono, Kartell, ICF,
Knoll, and more.

Vitra Design Museum
204 Pennsylvania Avenue,
Suite B
Easton, MD 21601
410-763-7698
www.vitra.com
Designs for the home from
Gehry, Thiel, Nelson,
Eames, and others.

Antiques & vintage-style pieces

ABC Carpet & Home
881–888 Broadway
New York, NY 10003
212-674-1144
www.abccarpet.com
Home furnishings, fabrics,
carpets, and design
accessories.

**American Pottery
Exchange**
www.the-apx.com
Popular ceramics; includes
Lu Ray, Russel Wright, Eva
Zeisel, McCoy, Bauer, and
many more.

Depot Antique Mall
8313 State Hwy 23
St. Cloud, MN 56301
320-253-6573
www.depot-antique-
  mall.com
A multi-dealer antique
mall in a historic
railroad depot.

EBay (Internet auctions)
www.ebay.com
Individual sellers, quality and prices vary, with every category of merchandise represented.

English Country Antiques
Snake Hollow Road
Bridgehampton
NY 11932
516-537-0606
Period country furniture in pine, plus decorative blue-and-white china.

Fishs Eddy
889 Broadway
New York, NY 10011
212-420-2090
Overstock supplies of Fifties-style china mugs, plates, bowls, etc.

Kitchen Sink Antiques
North Carolina 27613
www.kitchensink
   antiques.com
Specializes in all periods of glassware, dinnerware, kitchenware, restaurant china, and pottery.

Ladybug's Antiques and Collectibles
P.O. Box 574
Crystal City, MO 63019
www.tias.com/stores/lbac/
Selling a selection of glassware and pottery, with an emphasis on American pieces.

Once Upon a Table
Owner: Carol Levison
30 Crofut Street
Pittsfield, MA 01201
413-443-6622
www.onceuponatable.com
European and American period kitchenware; jadeite, Bakelite, FireKing, biscuit bins, and more.

Restoration Hardware
935 Broadway
New York, NY 10011
212-260-9479
www.restoration
   hardware.com
Not just hardware, but reproduction furnishings and knicknacks for the home and garden.

Ruby Beets Antiques
Poxybogue Road
Bridgehampton
NY 11932
516-537-2802
Antique painted furniture, old china, and kitchenware.

Tri-State Antique Center
47 West Pike
Canonsburg, PA 15317
724-745-9116
www.tristateantiques.com
Specializes in Heywood-Wakefield, mid-century modern furniture, and pottery, china, and glass.

Up The Creek's
American Antique Furniture Market
120 South Tower
Centralia, WA 98531
360-330-0427
www.amerantfurn.com
American furniture and lighting in Victorian, Eastlake, turn-of-the-century, Mission, Arts and Crafts, Depression and 1940s Classic Revival periods in both restored and original finish.

Victor DiPaola Antiques
Long Island, NY
516-488-5868
www.dipaolaantiques.com
Furniture and decorative arts of the 18th and 19th centuries.

A listing of over 40,000 antiques shops throughout the country exists at **www.curioscape.com.**

Flea markets

Alameda Swap Meet
Located on South Alameda Blvd.
Los Angeles, CA 90021
213-233-2764
Well-known, wide selection; held 7 days a week from 10 a.m. to 7 p.m. year round, 400 vendors.

Aunt Tinker's General Store
Highway 19
Big Spring, MO 63363
573-252-4707
Known for its unusual collectibles, this market is open daily from 10 a.m. to 5 p.m.

Brimfield Antique Show
Route 20
Brimfield, MA 01010
413-245-3436
www.brimfieldshow.com
Renowned as the Outdoor Antiques Capital of the World, this show is held for a week in the months of May, July, and September.

Denver Indoor Antique Market
1212 South Broadway
Denver, CO 80210
303-744-7049
Open seven days a week.

Merriam Lane Flea Market
14th and Merriam Lane
Kansas City, KS 66106
913-677-0833
Open-air market where estates are bought and sold; operates weekly in spring and summer from 7 a.m. to dark.

Ruth's Flea Market
Highway 431
Roanoke, AL 36274
334-864-7328
Over 300 booths selling all types of collectibles, new and old; weekly on Wednesdays and Saturdays.

Sullivan Flea Market
Heights Ravenna Road
5 Miles West of Ravenna Center
Ravenna, MI 49451
616-853-2435
Antiques, collectibles, fresh produce, and consignment; weekly on Mondays from April to the end of October.

Tesuque Pueblo Flea Market
Route 5
Santa Fe, NM 87501
505-660-8948
Native American crafts, antiques, rugs, collectibles, and southwest furniture, both new and used; monthly Friday to Sunday. Call to verify specific dates.

Traders Village (Houston)
Eldridge Road
Houston, TX 77083
713-890-5500
Largest market on the Texas Gulf coast, with over 800 dealers; Saturday and Sunday, 8 a.m. to 6 p.m., year-round.

Vintage Village
I-77 and U.S. Highway
Hamptonville, NC 27020
910-468-8616
New and old collectibles; Fridays 10 a.m.–4 p.m., and Saturdays and Sundays 8 a.m. to 5 p.m.

For listings of flea markets held throughout the country, go to **www.fleamarket guide.com**

picture credits

KEY: *ph*=photographer, **a**=above, **b**=below, **r**=right, **l**=left, **c**=center

Endpapers *ph* Alan Williams/Lindsay Taylor's apartment in Glasgow; **1** *ph* Polly Wreford/Adria Ellis's apartment in New York; **2–3** *ph* Tom Leighton/Keith Varty & Alan Cleaver's apartment in London, designed by Jonathan Reed/Reed Creative Services Ltd (+44 20 7565 0066); **4l** *ph* Polly Wreford/Daniel Jasiak's apartment in Paris; **4r** *ph* Polly Wreford/Ann Shore's house in London; **5** *ph* Polly Wreford/Glenn Carwithen & Sue Miller's house in London, painting by Alan Grimwood; **6** *ph* Tom Leighton; **8–9** *ph* Tom Leighton; **10–11** *ph* Polly Wreford/ Glenn Carwithen & Sue Miller's house in London; **12 & 13r** *ph* Tom Leighton; **13al** *ph* Ray Main/client's residence, East Hampton, New York, designed by ZG DESIGN; **13bl** *ph* Polly Wreford/Mary Foley's house in Connecticut; **14a** *ph* Polly Wreford/Lena Proudlock's house in Gloucestershire; **14b** *ph* Chris Everard/interior designer Ann Boyd's own apartment in London; **15** *ph* Polly Wreford/The Sawmills Studios; **16–17** *ph* Tom Leighton; **17** *ph* Chris Everard/François Muracciole's apartment in Paris; **18** *ph* Ray Main/Gisela Garson's house in Stoke Newington, designed by FAT; **18–19** *ph* Ray Main/David Mellor's home and studio at Hathersage in Derbyshire; **20l both** *ph* Alan Williams/ Katie Bassford King's house in London, designed by Touch Interior Design; **20r** *ph* Polly Wreford/Clare Nash's house in London; **21** *ph* Verity Welstead/Lulu Guinness's house in London; **22, 23l & 23ar** *ph* Andrew Wood/ Norma Holland's house in London; **23br** *ph* Polly Wreford/Ros Fairman's house in London; **24–25a** *ph* Ray Main/Evan Snyderman's house in Brooklyn; **24bl** *ph* Polly Wreford/an apartment in New York, designed by Belmont Freeman Architects; **24–25b** *ph* Polly Wreford/home of 27.12 Design Ltd, Chelsea, NYC; **26a** *ph* Tom Leighton/ interior designer Philip Hooper's own house in East Sussex; **26b** *ph* Jan Baldwin/interior designer Philip Hooper's own house in East Sussex; **27** *ph* Ray Main/ Thierry Watorek's house near Paris; **28–29** *ph* Ray Main/ Greville & Sophie Worthington's home in Yorkshire; **30l** *ph* Catherine Gratwicke/Intérieurs in New York; **30r both** *ph* Andrew Wood/Roger & Fay Oates's house in Eastnor, Herefordshire; **31** *ph* Catherine Gratwicke/an apartment in Paris, designed by Bruno Tanquerel; **32–33** *ph* Polly Wreford; **33al** *ph* Tom Leighton; **33cl&bl** *ph* Polly Wreford; **33ar** *ph* Catherine Gratwicke/ Martin Barrell & Amanda Sellers's flat, owners of Maisonette, London; **33bc&br** *ph* Tom Leighton; **34–35** *ph* Thomas Stewart/The T House in London,

designed by Ian Chee of VX Design; **35al** *ph* Catherine Gratwicke/Frances Robinson & Eamonn McMahon's house in London; **35ac&ar** *ph* Polly Wreford/an apartment in New York, designed by Belmont Freeman Architects; **35bl** *ph* Polly Wreford/home of 27.12 Design Ltd, Chelsea, NYC; **35br** *ph* Tom Leighton; **36** *ph* James Merrell; **37** *ph* Andrew Wood/Norma Holland's house in London; **38al** *ph* Ray Main/Marie-Pierre Morel's house in Paris, designed by François Muracciole; **38bl** *ph* Chris Everard/Eric De Queker's apartment in Antwerp; **38–39** *ph* Ray Main/Kenneth Hirst's apartment in New York; **39** *ph* Polly Wreford/Carol Reid's apartment in Paris; **40l** *ph* Chris Everard/François Muracciole's apartment in Paris; **40r & 41** *ph* James Merrell/Christine Walsh & Ian Bartlett's house in London, designed by Jack Ingham of Bookworks; **42** *ph* Polly Wreford/Ros Fairman's house in London; **43l** *ph* Alan Williams/interior designer and managing director of the Société Yves Halard, Michelle Halard's own apartment in Paris; **43ar** *ph* Polly Wreford/The Sawmills Studios; **43br** *ph* Chris Everard/François Muracciole's apartment in Paris; **44al** *ph* Tom Leighton; **44r** *ph* Chris Everard/an apartment in Milan, designed by Nicoletta Marazza; **44bl** *ph* Tom Leighton/paint Farrow & Ball: floor Mouse's Back floor paint no. 40, cupboards Green Smoke no. 47 and interior Red Fox no. 48, walls and woodwork String no. 8, ceiling Off White no. 3; **45** *ph* James Merrell/Sally Butler's house in London; **46 & 47ar** *ph* James Merrell/Ash Sakula's house in London; **47al** *ph* James Merrell/Stephen Woodhams's house in London, designed in conjunction with Mark Brook Design; **47cr** *ph* James Merrell; **47br** *ph* James Merrell/John Alexander & Fiona Waterstreet's loft in New York, designed by Lorraine Kirke; **48l both** *ph* Catherine Gratwicke/Lulu Guinness's home in London; **48r & 49** *ph* Catherine Gratwicke/ Agnès Emery's house in Brussels; tiles, star light and drawer handles from Emery & Cie; **50** *ph* Catherine Gratwicke/Etienne & Mary Millner's house in London, ceramics from Selfridges; **51al&bl** *ph* Catherine Gratwicke; **51r** *ph* Catherine Gratwicke/The Jeff McKay Inc. advertising and public relations agency in New York, designed by David Mann & James Corbett; **52** *ph* Andrew Wood; **53l** *ph* Chris Everard/an apartment in London, designed by Jo Hagan of USE Architects; **53r both** *ph* Andrew Wood/Heidi Kingstone's apartment in London; **54al** *ph* Polly Wreford/an apartment in New York, designed by Belmont Freeman Architects;

54bl&br *ph* Tom Leighton/a loft in London, designed by Robert Dye Associates, chairs Twentieth Century Design, wooden containers David Wainwright, bamboo plates, bowl and ceramic bowls David Champion; **54–55** *ph* Andrew Wood/Norma Holland's house in London; **55r** *ph* Andrew Wood/Chelsea loft apartment in New York, designed by The Moderns; **56** *ph* Polly Wreford/The Sawmills Studios; **57a both** *ph* James Merrell/John Alexander & Fiona Waterstreet's loft in New York designed by Lorraine Kirke; **57cl&br** *ph* Andrew Wood/the home of Gwen Aldridge & Bruce McLucas; **57bl** *ph* Polly Wreford/Glenn Carwithen & Sue Miller's house in London; **57bc** *ph* James Merrell/Ash Sakula's house in London; **58** *ph* Chris Everard/an apartment in Milan, designed by Daniela Micol Wajskol, interior designer, kitchen table and chairs from Polenghi Antiquario, Milan; **59al** *ph* Andrew Wood/Norma Holland's house in London; **59ar** *ph* Verity Welstead/Lulu Guinness's house in London; **59bl** *ph* Andrew Wood/the Pasadena, California, home of Susan D'Avignon; **59bc** *ph* Ray Main/Thierry Watorek's house near Paris; **59br** *ph* Andrew Wood/media executive's house in Los Angeles, architect: Stephen Slan, builder: Ken Duran, furnishings: Russell Simpson, original architect: Carl Maston c. 1945; **60–61** *ph* Alan Williams/Katie Bassford King's house in London, designed by Touch Interior Design; **62** *ph* Polly Wreford/Adria Ellis's apartment in New York, painting by Peter Zangrillo; **63al** *ph* Henry Bourne; **63bl** *ph* Andrew Wood/John Cheim's apartment in New York; **63r** *ph* Tom Leighton; **64l** *ph* Tom Leighton; **64r** *ph* Polly Wreford/Lena Proudlock's house in Gloucestershire; **65** *ph* Polly Wreford/The Sawmills Studios; **66** *ph* Polly Wreford/Glenn Carwithen & Sue Miller's house in London; **67a** *ph* Tom Leighton; **67b** *ph* Polly Wreford/Clare Nash's house in London; **68a&bl** *ph* Polly Wreford/Ros Fairman's house in London; **68br** *ph* Catherine Gratwicke; **69** *ph* Polly Wreford/Mary Foley's house in Connecticut; **70–71 & 71al** *ph* Andrew Wood/media executive's house in Los Angeles, architect: Stephen Slan, builder: Ken Duran, furnishings: Russell Simpson, original architect: Carl Maston c. 1945; **71r both** *ph* Andrew Wood/Kurt Bredenbeck's apartment at the Barbican, London; **72** *ph* Catherine Gratwicke/the brownstone in New York of Bonnie Young, director of global sourcing and inspiration at Donna Karan International; **73** *ph* Tom Leighton/Keith Varty & Alan Cleaver's apartment in London, designed by Jonathan Reed/Reed Creative Services Ltd (+44 20 7565 0066); **74** *ph* Henry Bourne; **75al** *ph* Polly Wreford/Ros Fairman's house in London; **75ar** *ph* Polly Wreford/home of 27.12 Design Ltd, Chelsea, NYC; **75bl** *ph* Alan Williams/the architect Voon Wong's own apartment in London; **75br** *ph* Andrew Wood/Heidi Kingstone's apartment in London; **76–77** *ph* Alan Williams/owner of Gloss, Pascale Bredillet's own apartment in London; **77al&ac** *ph* Polly Wreford; **77ar** *ph* Polly Wreford/Clare Nash's house in London; **77bl** *ph* Polly Wreford/Ros Fairman's house in London; **77br** *ph* Polly Wreford; **78–79** *ph* Andrew Wood/Alastair Hendy & John Clinch's apartment in London, designed by Alastair Hendy; **80 & 81al** *ph* Alan Williams/Katie Bassford King's house in London, designed by Touch Interior Design; **81ar** *ph* Catherine Gratwicke/Ellis Flyte's house in London; **81br** *ph* Ray Main/Kirk & Caroline Pickering's house in London, space creation by Square Foot Properties Ltd; **82l** *ph* Andrew Wood/Alastair Hendy & John Clinch's apartment in London, designed by Alastair Hendy; **82r all** *ph* Andrew Wood/a house in London, designed by Bowles & Linares; **83** *ph* Polly Wreford/an apartment in New York, designed by Belmont Freeman Architects; **84 & 85bl** *ph* Ray Main/Jonathan Leitersdorf's apartment in New York, designed by Jonathan Leitersdorf/Just Design Ltd; **85al&cl** *ph* Catherine Gratwicke/the brownstone in New York of Bonnie Young, director of global sourcing and inspiration at Donna Karan International; **85ar** *ph* Chris Everard/an apartment in Milan, designed by Nicoletta Marazza; **85br** *ph* Chris Everard/Sera Hersham-Loftus' house in London; **86al** *ph* Chris Everard/Gentucca Bini's apartment in Milan; **86ac&ar** *ph* Chris Everard/Lulu Guinness's house in London; **86bl** *ph* Chris Everard/Florence Buchanan, Steve Harrison & Octavia Spelman's house, Tribeca, New York, designed by Sage Wimer Coombe Architects; **86br** *ph* Chris Everard/Suzanne Slesin & Michael Steinberg's apartment in New York, designed by Jean-Louis Ménard; **87** *ph* Polly Wreford/Ros Fairman's house in London; **88–89** *ph* Ray Main/Marina & Peter Hill's barn in West Sussex, designed by Marina Hill, Peter James Construction Management, Chichester, The West Sussex Antique Timber Company, Wisborough Green, and Joanna Jefferson Architects; **90a both** *ph* Chris Everard/Mark Kirkley & Harumi Kaijima's house in Sussex; **90b** *ph* Jan Baldwin/a house in Maine designed by Stephen Blatt Architects; **91** *ph* Tom Leighton/Roger & Fay Oates's house in Eastnor, Herefordshire; **92** *ph* Andrew Wood/a house in London designed by Bowles & Linares; **93al&bc** *ph* Chris Everard/Sera Hersham-Loftus' house in London; **93ar&br** *ph* Chris Everard/Suzanne Slesin & Michael Steinberg's apartment in New York, design by Jean-Louis Ménard; **93bl** *ph* Andrew Wood/Roger & Fay Oates's house in Eastnor, Herefordshire; **94–95** *ph* Alan Williams/owner of Gloss, Pascale Bredillet's own apartment in London; **96–97** *ph* Polly Wreford/Daniel Jasiak's apartment in Paris; **98l** *ph* Ray Main/Evan Snyderman's house in Brooklyn; **98ar** *ph* Tom Leighton; **98br** *ph* Verity Welstead/Alison & Paul Holberton's house in Southwark, London; **99al** *ph* Andrew Wood/Mary Shaw's Sequana apartment in Paris; **99ar** *ph* Polly Wreford/Kathy Moskal's apartment in New York, designed by Ken Foreman; **99b** *ph* James Merrell; **100bl** *ph* Andrew Wood/Neil Bingham's house in Blackheath, London, chair from Designer's Guild; **100ar** *ph* Andrew Wood/Century (+44 20 7487 5100); **100br** *ph* Tom Leighton; **101al** *ph* Catherine Gratwicke/a New York City apartment, designed by Marino + Giolito; **101bl** *ph* Andrew Wood/Brian Johnson's apartment in London, designed by Johnson Naylor, chairs courtesy of Race Furniture; **101bc** *ph* Andrew Wood/Century (+44 20 7487 5100); **101ar** *ph* Andrew Wood/Ian Chee's apartment in London, chair courtesy of Vitra; **101br** *ph* Tom Leighton/interior designer Philip Hooper's own house in East Sussex; **102al** *ph* Polly Wreford/The Sawmills Studios; **102–103a** *ph* Tom Leighton; **102b & 103 all** *ph* Tom Leighton; **104** *ph* Andrew Wood/Ian Bartlett & Christine Walsh's house in London; **104–105** *ph* Andrew Wood; **105ar** *ph* Tom Leighton; **105b** *ph* Ray Main; **106l** *ph* Andrew Wood/a house in London, designed by Guy Stansfeld (+44 20 7727 0133); **106r** *ph* Tom Leighton; **107al** *ph* Tom Leighton; **107b** *ph* Andrew Wood/the London flat of Miles Johnson & Frank Ronan; **107r** *ph* Andrew Wood; **108l** *ph* Catherine Gratwicke/Kimball Mayer & Meghan Hughes's apartment in New York, designed by L.A. Morgan; **108r** *ph* Polly Wreford/an apartment in New York, designed by Belmont Freeman Architects; **109b** *ph* Catherine Gratwicke/Sean & Mary Kelly's loft in New York, designed by Steven Learner; **109a** *ph* Polly Wreford/home of 27.12 Design Ltd, Chelsea, NYC; **110l** *ph* Tom Leighton; **110r** *ph* Catherine Gratwicke/Elena Colombo's apartment in New York; **111l** *ph* Tom Leighton; **111ar** *ph* Catherine Gratwicke/Johanne Riss's house in Brussels; **111br** *ph* Tom Leighton/paint Paint Library, chair fabric Livingstone Studio, lamp Valerie Wade, artwork by Zoë Hope, table Josephine Ryan; **112–113** *ph* Alan Williams/Géraldine Prieur's apartment in Paris, an interior designer fascinated with colour; **114l&ar** *ph* Andrew Wood/Phillip Low, New York; **114br** *ph* Catherine Gratwicke; **114–115** *ph* Polly Wreford/Ann Shore's house in London; **115a** *ph* Polly Wreford; **115b** *ph* Fritz von der Schulenburg; **116al** *ph* Andrew Wood; **116bl** *ph* Polly Wreford; **116r & 117al** *ph* Andrew Wood/Guido Palau's house in north London, designed by Azman Owens Architects; **117bl** *ph* Chris Everard/Reuben Barrett's apartment in London, light from Mathmos; **117ar** *ph* Andrew Wood/an apartment in The San Remo on the Upper West Side of Manhattan, designed by John L. Stewart and Michael D'Arcy of SIT; **117br** *ph* Chris Everard/light courtesy of Skandium; **118–119** *ph* Andrew Wood/Chelsea loft apartment in New York, designed by The Moderns; **120al,acl,ar&bl all** *ph* Polly Wreford; **120acr** *ph* James Merrell; **120br** *ph* Verity Welstead; **121** *ph* Tom Leighton; **122** *ph* Andrew Wood/Mary Shaw's Sequana apartment in Paris; **123al&bl** *ph* James Merrell; **123cl** *ph* Polly Wreford; **123r** *ph* Henry Bourne; **124al** *ph* Andrew Wood/Chelsea loft apartment in New York, designed by The Moderns; **124bl** *ph* Andrew Wood/Jane Collins of Sixty 6 in Marylebone High Street, home in central London; **124ca&b** *ph* Andrew Wood; **124r** *ph* Polly Wreford; **125** *ph* Andrew Wood/Jo Shane, John Cooper & family, apartment in New York; **125 inset** *ph* Andrew Wood/Chelsea loft apartment in New York, designed by The Moderns; **126–127** *ph* Polly Wreford/home of 27.12 Design Ltd, Chelsea, NYC; **128 & 129l** *ph* Polly Wreford/Clare Nash's house in London; **129ar** *ph* Polly Wreford/Ros Fairman's house in London; **129br** *ph* Chris Everard; **130a** *ph* Catherine Gratwicke/Jonathan Adler & Simon Doonan's apartment in New York; **130–131b & 131b** *ph* Alan Williams/director of design consultants Graven Images, Janice Kirkpatrick's apartment in Glasgow; **131al** *ph* Catherine Gratwicke/Kari Sigerson's apartment in New York; **131ac&ar** *ph* Tom Leighton; **132** *ph* Tham Nhu-Tran; **133** *ph* Polly Wreford; **134al** *ph* Catherine Gratwicke/Martin Barrell & Amanda Sellers's flat, owners of Maisonette, London; **134bl** *ph* Thomas Stewart; **134r** *ph* Polly Wreford; **135l** *ph* Polly Wreford/Clare Nash's house in London; **135 ar&b** *ph* Tham Nhu-Tran/Ian Chee's house in London; **136al** *ph* David Brittain; **136ar&b** *ph* Tom Leighton; **137l** *ph* Tom Leighton/Roger & Fay Oates's house in Eastnor, Herefordshire; **137r** *ph* Tom Leighton.

Publisher's acknowledgments: In addition to the designers, architects, and home owners mentioned above, the publishers would also like to thank Netty Nauta, Aleid Rontgen and Annette Brederode, designers Roxanne Beis and Jean-Bernard Navier, Caroline and Michael Breet, Marilyn Phipps, Shiraz Maneksha, Glen Senk and Brian Johnson of Anthropologie, Potted Gardens, Tricia Foley, George Laaland at Woolloomooloo Restaurant, and Angela Miller & Russell Glover.

Author's acknowledgments: I'd like to thank my family, friends, and colleagues for their constant and unstinting support, advice, and help while I was writing this book.

architects & designers

KEY: *a*=above, *b*=below, *r*=right, *l*=left, *c*=center

Jonathan Adler
465 Broome Street
New York, NY 10013
t. 212 941 8950
Page 116a

Anthropologie
375 West Broadway
New York, NY 10012
Pages 63r, 107bl

Ash Sakula Architects
24 Rosebery Avenue
London EC1R 4SX
UK
t. +44 20 7837 9735
f. +44 20 7837 9708
e. robert@ashsak.com
www.ashsak.com
Pages 46, 47ar, 57bc

Azman Owens Architects
Architects
8 St Albans Place
London NW1 0NX
UK
t. +44 20 7354 2955
f. +44 20 7354 2966
Pages 116r, 117al

Belmont Freeman Architects
Project team: Belmont
Freeman (principal designer),
Alane Truitt
Sangho Park
110 West 40th Street
New York, NY 10018
t. 212 382 3311
f. 212 730 1229
*Pages 24bl, 35ac, 35ar, 54ar,
83, 108r*

Stephen Blatt Architects
Architectural Design Firm
10 Danforth Street
Portland, Maine 04101
t. 207 761 5911
f. 207 761 2105
e. sba@sbarchitects.com
Page 90b

Bowles & Linares
32 Hereford Road
London W2 5AJ
UK
t. +44 20 7229 9886
Pages 82r all, 92

Ann Boyd Design Ltd
33 Elystan Street
London SW3 3NT
UK
t. +44 20 7591 0202
Page 14b

Annette Brederode
(by appointment only)
Lynbaansgracht 56d
Amsterdam
Holland
Pages 8–9, 102–103a

Caroline Breet
Caroline's Antiek & Brocante
Nieuweweg 35A
251 LH Laren
Holland
Pages 16–17

Mark Brook Design
7 Sunderland Terrace
London W2 5PA
UK
t. +44 20 7221 8106
Page 47al

Elena Colombo
Sculptor and designer
e. eacolombo@earthlink.net
Page 110r

Eric De Queker
DQ Design In Motion
Koninklijkelaan 44
2600 Bercham
Belgium
Page 38bl

Robert Dye Associates
68–74 Rochester Place
London NW1 9JX
Pages 54bl, 54cr, 54br

Emery & Cie and Noir D'Ivorie
25–29 rue de l'Hôpital
Brussels
Belgium
t. +32 2 513 5892
f. +32 5 513 3970
Pages 48r, 49

FAT
Appletree Cottage
116–120 Golden Lane
London EC1Y 0TL
UK
t. +44 20 7251 6735
f. +44 20 7251 6730
e. fat@fat.co.uk
www.fat.co.uk
Page 18

Ellis Flyte
Fashion designer
f. +44 20 7431 7560
Page 81ar

Ken Foreman
Architect
105 Duane Street
New York, NY 10007
t.&f. 212 924 4503
Page 99ar

Gloss Ltd
Home accessories
274 Portobello Road
London W10 5TE
UK
t. +44 20 8960 4146
f. +44 20 8960 4842
e. pascale@gloss
   ltd.u-net.com
Pages 76–77, 94–95

Russell Glover
Architect
e. russellglover@earthlink.net
Pages 120acr, 123al

Lulu Guinness
3 Ellis Street
London SW1X 9AL
UK
t. +44 20 7823 4828
f. +44 20 7823 4889
www.luluguinness.com
Pages 21, 48l, 59ar, 86ac, 86ar

Yves Halard
Interior decoration
27 quai de la Tournelle
75005 Paris
France
t. +33 1 44 07 14 00
f. +33 1 44 07 10 30
Page 43al

Alastair Hendy
Food writer, art director,
and designer
f. +44 20 7739 6040
Pages 78–79, 82l

Sera Hersham-Loftus
"Rude" designer and
lampshade maker
t. +44 20 7286 5948
Pages 85b, 93al, 93bc

Hirst Pacific Ltd
250 Lafayette Street
New York, NY 10012
t. 212 625 3670
f. 212 625 3673
e. hirstpacific@earthlink.net
Pages 38–39

Philip Hooper
Interior designer
Studio 30
The Old Latchmere School
38 Barns Road
London SW11 5GY
UK
t. +44 20 7978 6662
f. +44 20 7223 3713
Pages 26, 101br

Jack Ingham
Bookworks
34 Ansleigh Place
London W11 4BW
UK
t. +44 20 7792 8310
Pages 40r, 41

Intérieurs
114 Wooster Street
New York, NY 10012
Page 30l

Daniel Jasiak
Designer
12 rue Jean Ferrandi
Paris 75006
France
t. +33 1 45 49 13 56
f. +33 1 45 49 23 66
Pages 4l, 96–97

Joanna Jefferson Architects
222 Oving Road
Chichester
West Sussex PO19 4EJ
UK
t. +44 1243 532398
f. +44 1243 531550
e. jjeffearch@aol.com
Pages 88–89

Johnson Naylor
13 Britton Street
London EC1M 5SX
UK
t. +44 20 7490 8885
f. +44 20 7490 0038
Page 101bc

Just Design Ltd
80 5th Avenue
18th Floor
New York, NY 10011
t. 212 243 6544
f. 212 229 1112
e. wbp@angel.net
Pages 84, 85bl

Sean Kelly Gallery
528 West 29th Street
New York, NY 10001
t. 212 239 1181
f. 212 239 2467
www.skny.com
Page 109b

Mark Kirkley
Designer & manufacturer
of interior metalwork
t.&f. +44 1424 812613
Page 90a both

Steven Learner Studio
Architecture and interior
design
307 7th Avenue
New York, NY 10001
t. 212 741 8583
f. 212 741 2180
e. info@stevenlearnerstudio.com
www.stevenlearnerstudio.com
Page 109b

Maisonette
79 Chamberlayne Road
London NW10 3ND
UK
t. +44 20 8964 8444
f. +44 20 8964 8464
e. maisonetteUK@aol.com
Pages 33ar, 134al

David Mann
MR Architecture + Décor
150 West 28th Street, 1102
New York, NY 10001
t. 212 989 9300
f. 212 989 9430
e. MANN@MRARCH.COM
James Corbett can be
contacted through David Mann
Page 51r

Nicoletta Marazza
via G Morone, 8
20121 Milan
Italy
t.&f. +39 2 7601 4482
Pages 44r, 85ar

Marino + Giolito
161 West 16th Street
New York, NY 10011
t.&f. 212 675 5737
Page 101al

Jeff McKay Inc.
Advertising and PR agency
203 Lafayette Street
New York, NY 10012
t. 212 771 1770
Page 51r

David Mellor Design
Hathersage
Sheffield S32 1BA
UK
t. +44 1433 650 220
f. +44 1433 650 944
e. davidmellor@ukonline.co.uk
Pages 18–19

Jean-Louis Ménard
32 boulevard de l'Hôpital
75005 Paris
France
t. +33 43 36 31 74
Pages 86br, 93ar, 93br

The Moderns
900 Broadway, Suite 903
New York, NY 10003
t. 212 387 8852
f. 212 387 8824
e. moderns@aol.com
*Page 55r, 118, 119, 124al,
125 inset*

L.A. Morgan
Interior designer
P O Box 39
Hadlyme
CT 06439
t. 860 434 0304
f. 860 434 3013
Page 108l

François Muracciole
Architect
54 rue de Montreuil
75011 Paris
France
t. +33 1 43 71 33 03
e. francois.muracciole
@libertysurf.fr
Pages 17, 38al, 40l, 43br

Roger Oates Design
Shop & showroom:
1 Munro Terrace
Chelsea
London SW10 0DL
Studio shop:
The Long Barn
Eastnor
Ledbury
Herefordshire HR8 1EL
UK
Pages 30r both, 91, 93bl, 137l

Géraldine Prieur
Interior designer
7 rue Faraday
75017 Paris
France
t. +33 1 44 40 29 12
f. +33 1 44 40 29 17
Pages 112, 113

Lena Proudlock
Denim in Style
Drews House
Leighterton
Gloucestershire GL8 8UN
UK
t.&f. +44 1666 890230
Pages 14a, 64r

Reed Creative Services Ltd
151a Sydney Street
London SW3 6NT
UK
t. +44 20 7565 0066
Pages 2–3, 73

Johanne Riss
Stylist, designer, and
fashion designer
35 place du Nouveau Marché
aux Graens
1000 Brussels
Belgium
t. +32 2 513 0900
f. +32 2 514 3284
Page 111ar

Frances Robinson
Detail jewelry designers
and consultants
t. +44 20 7582 9564
f. +44 20 7587 3783
Page 35al

Sage Wimer Coombe
Architects
Project team: Jennifer Sage,
Peter Coombe, Suzan Selcuk,
Peggy Tan
480 Canal Street, Room 1002
New York, NY 10013
t. 212 226 9600
Page 86bl

Sequana
64 avenue de la Motte Picquet
75015 Paris
France
t. +33 1 45 66 58 40
f. +33 1 45 67 99 81
e. sequana@wandoo.fr
Pages 99al, 122 all

Ann Shore
Story
(by appointment only)
t.&f. +44 20 7377 6377
Pages 4r, 114–115

Stephen Slan AIA
Variations In Architecture Inc.
2156 Hollyridge Drive
Los Angeles
California 90068
t. 323 467 4455
f. 323 467 6655
Pages 59br, 70–71, 71al

Square Foot Properties Ltd
50 Britton Street
London EC1M 5UP
UK
t. +44 20 7253 2527
f. +44 20 7253 2528
Page 81br

John L. Stewart
SIT, LLC
113–115 Bank Street
New York, NY 10014
t. 212 620 777
f. 212 620 0770
e. JLSCollection@aol.com
Page 117ar

Bruno Tanquerel
Artist
2 passage St. Sébastien
75011 Paris
France
t. +33 1 43 57 03 93
Page 31

Touch Interior Design
t. +44 20 7498 6409
Pages 20l both, 60, 61, 80, 81al

USE Architects
11 Northburgh Street
London EC1V 0AH
UK
t. +44 20 7251 5559
f. +44 20 7253 5558
e. use.arch@virgin.net
Page 53l

VX Design & Architecture
e. vx@vxdesign.com
www.vxdesign.com
*Pages 34–35, 101ar, 135ar,
135b*

Voon Wong Architects
Unit 27, 1 Stannary Street
London SW11 4AD
UK
t. +44 20 7587 0116
f. +44 20 7840 0178
e. voon@dircon.co.uk
Page 75bl

Woodhams Ltd
t. +44 20 8964 9818
Page 47al

Bonnie Young
Director of global sourcing and
inspiration at Donna Karan
International
t. 212 228 0832
Pages 72, 85al, 85ac

ZG Design
10 Wireless Road
East Hampton
NY 11937
t. 631 329 7486
f. 631 329 2087
e. dzina@ATT.net
www.zgdesign.com
Page 13al

27.12 Design Ltd
451 Greenwich Street, Suite 504
New York, NY 10013
t. 212 334 5245
*Pages 24–25b, 35bl, 75ar, 109a,
126–127*

INDEX

Page numbers in *italic* refer to captions